Modernising Scientific Careers in Physics and Engineering:
Seventh Edition: December 2023

Many thanks must go to Rachel Ganney who foolishly offered to turn these lecture notes into a book.

Also to Sandhya Pisharody, Phil Cosgriff, Allan Green, Richard Trouncer and David Willis who co-authored material adapted (closely in some cases) for this book.

With a grateful nod to Patrick Williams, Henry Morton and Cliff Ruff whose assistance with the practical group work that formed an important part of the course on which this book is based was invaluable. Very grateful thanks to Claire Hardiman, who suggested the course in the first place.

Published by: Eternal Sound and Light, Tenerife

Modernising Scientific Careers in Physics and Engineering: the ICT competencies

Paul Ganney, Mark White & Patrick Maw
Edited by Rachel Ganney

Contents

Introduction

Modernising Scientific Careers is the umbrella name for delivering scientific training to the healthcare workforce. Six of the seven Medical Physics and Clinical Engineering themes contain a substantive amount of ICT knowledge and expertise to be delivered in the workplace (Rehabilitation Engineering is the exception). This book covers the MSC workplace syllabus for the Medical Physics themes (Ionising Radiation, Non-Ionising Radiation, Radiotherapy, Radiation Protection). It also covers the ICT competencies for the Clinical Engineering theme of Clinical Measurement & Development and most of them for Device Risk Management & Governance[i].

In 2013 we decided to deliver this material via a 4-day training course. The material in this book is based upon the latest version of those lectures. As such it does not contain the asides, bad jokes, solutions to questions, rumours, anecdotes or group exercises from the course[ii].

Nomenclature

Text in *italics* is usually a quotation, especially from standards and legislation.

Text in **bold** is usually the first use of a word or phrase that is subsequently abbreviated. All such abbreviations are listed in Appendix 1.

References are [1] and are listed in Appendix 3.

Footnotes are denoted [i] and appear at the foot of the page.

---

[i] Those omitted are "Apply engineering principles to classify and structure the institution's approach to medical device categorisation" and "Design, produce and utilise key performance indicators for use in performance management of the medical device risk management and governance service".

[ii] Well, some of them may have escaped editing.

Chapter 1 – Information Governance

Information Governance (IG) is the function of corporate governance that ensures the confidentiality, integrity and availability of an organisation's information assets.

There is a range of complex legal and professional obligations that limit, prohibit or set conditions in respect of the management, use and disclosure of information and, similarly, a range of statutes that permit or require information to be used or disclosed. The NHS document "NHS Information Governance - Guidance on Legal and Professional Obligations" lists 44 pieces of relevant legislation, 14 standards and guidelines and 8 professional codes of conduct[1], but the **General Data Protection Regulation** (GDPR), **Freedom of Information Act** (FOI) and Caldicott reviews are the only three of these that we'll cover here.

IG is achieved through a mix of policy and protocol. It is not unusual for IG policies to form part of an employee's contract. The major tension in IG for Healthcare (and arguably any organisation) is between openness and confidentiality. Too confidential (restrictive) and the delivery of healthcare suffers; too open and patient confidentiality suffers (so might the financial integrity of the organisation which in turn would impact upon healthcare delivery: thus an imbalance results in reduced healthcare, whichever way the imbalance lies). There is also the tension of the adoption of leading edge technology without introducing unacceptable levels of risk – the protocols must be open enough to permit this advance, whilst being restrictive enough to prevent breaches.

IG protocols need to recognise the need to share information between health organisations and other agencies in a controlled manner consistent with the interests of the patient (and in some circumstances, the public interest). Underpinning this is the need for electronic and paper information to be accurate, relevant, and available when required and processed appropriately (otherwise the data does not form information – "Information = Data + Structure").

It is impossible to create policies which achieve complete restriction and complete openness. Therefore a large element of IG is in risk reduction: a pragmatic approach to ensuring the organisation can function and develop, without leaving it open to damage.

IG polices will cover all "Information Assets" which include all information and data held by the organisation, whether held electronically or in manual, paper based systems and all information processing/computer systems and networks owned or operated by the organisation including all systems operated on behalf of it by third parties and those entrusted to it by third parties (e.g. N3[i]).

All organisations will have an IG manager/officer/director who will have top-level (e.g. Executive Board) influence and authority. It is their responsibility to interpret legislation, devise the organisation's implementation of this and to advise and rule on risk.

Up until 2008, NHS Trusts had to make an **Information Governance Statement of Compliance** (IGSoC) which was part of the Connecting for Health IG Toolkit. This IGSoC declaration has now been superseded by the requirement in the IG Toolkit[ii] to accept the IG Assurance Statement. This is re-confirmed each year by the submission of the annual IG Toolkit Assessment.

Two systems are required to implement IG: Firstly, in order to monitor compliance, an organisation should have a reporting mechanism for incidents and this will most likely be as a part of an existing incident reporting system. Secondly, an Information Asset's inability to comply fully with policies and procedures does not necessarily mean it

---

[i] The secure network used by the NHS

[ii] The IG Toolkit is an online system which allows NHS organisations to assess themselves or be assessed against Information Governance policies and standards. It also allows members of the public to view participating organisations' IG Toolkit assessments.

cannot be deployed. However, it must be fully risk assessed and entered onto a risk register in order to do so (see page 51 for details).

Information Governance may include computer forensic readiness which is the ability of an organisation to maximise its potential to use digital evidence whilst minimising the costs of an investigation. This is normally utilised after an incident (criminal or otherwise) and may involve log files, emails, back-ups etc. which therefore need to be retrievable in a suitable interpretable format.

Part of the restriction IG implements comes under the heading "data security" and the NHS has adopted the BS ISO 27000 series of Information Security Standards[iii] which address this. Data security addresses:

- the physical security for data centres and communication/hub rooms
- technical measures/standards to achieve appropriate access control (e.g. password complexity and expiry)
- standards for the development of software
- standards for the procurement of software
- disaster recovery/business continuity standards
- technical standards and process to prevent malicious code attack (e.g. intrusion detection systems and anti-virus)
- standards for technical documentation etc.

Whilst IG can at first appear to be a restrictive mechanism and the role of the IG Manager one of bottleneck or killjoy, if implemented properly with all aspects of the organisation's activities considered, it can assist in releasing information, especially for research purposes. As such it should be regarded more as an enabler (by doing things properly and efficiently) than a disabler.

There are two main pieces of general legislation covering the use of information/data and the right to disclosure. Personal data is covered by the General Data Protection Regulation and official information by the Freedom of Information Act. A third item, the Environmental Information Regulations[2] (with a separate version for Scotland), covers more public bodies but is only likely to impact upon the NHS in terms of buildings and waste disposal, so we won't be considering it here (but if your specialism is Nuclear Medicine you might want to). The particular sensitivities surrounding medical data were considered by the first Caldicott committee in 1997 (Caldicott2: "'Information: To Share Or Not To Share?" was accepted by the Government in October 2013 and builds on this first work). We will first consider the legislation, then proceed to required practice within the medical environment.

The European Union General Data Protection Regulation (EU GDPR[iv])
This new regulation took effect on 25th May 2018. Although born in the EU, it has a broad reach and will affect many organisations around the globe, including a post-Brexit UK – partly because it is enshrined in UK law as the **Data Protection Act** (DPA) (2018), which replaced DPA 1998 enacted in 2000. It applies to processing carried out by organisations operating within the EU as well as organisations outside of the EU that offer goods or services to individuals in the EU. The GDPR does not apply to certain activities including processing covered by the Law Enforcement Directive[v], processing for national security purposes and processing carried out by individuals purely for personal/household activities.

[iii] BS ISO/IEC 27002:2013 Information technology - Security techniques - Code of practice for information security controls
BS ISO/IEC 27001:2013 Information technology - Security techniques - Information security management systems - Requirements
BS ISO/IEC 27005:2011 Information technology - Security techniques - Information security risk management
[iv] Although "EU GDPR" is the official title, it is more commonly referred to as "GDPR", which we will do from this point onwards.
[v] An EU directive that "*lays down the rules relating to the protection of natural persons with regard to the processing of personal data by competent authorities for the purposes of the prevention, investigation, detection or prosecution of criminal offences or*

The GDPR applies to controllers and processors. A controller determines the purposes and means of processing personal data (how and why), whereas a processor is responsible for processing this data on behalf of a controller. The GDPR places specific legal obligations on processors. For example, the requirement to maintain records of personal data and processing activities. Controllers are not relieved of their obligations when a processor is involved – the GDPR places further obligations on them to ensure that their contracts with processors comply with the GDPR. The GDPR has seven main principles, which are recorded in Article 5:

"1. Personal data shall be:

(a) processed lawfully, fairly and in a transparent manner in relation to the data subject ('lawfulness, fairness and transparency');

(b) collected for specified, explicit and legitimate purposes and not further processed in a manner that is incompatible with those purposes; further processing for archiving purposes in the public interest, scientific or historical research purposes or statistical purposes shall, in accordance with Article 89(1), not be considered to be incompatible with the initial purposes ('purpose limitation');

(c) adequate, relevant and limited to what is necessary in relation to the purposes for which they are processed ('data minimisation');

(d) accurate and, where necessary, kept up to date; every reasonable step must be taken to ensure that personal data that are inaccurate, having regard to the purposes for which they are processed, are erased or rectified without delay ('accuracy');

(e) kept in a form which permits identification of data subjects for no longer than is necessary for the purposes for which the personal data are processed; personal data may be stored for longer periods insofar as the personal data will be processed solely for archiving purposes in the public interest, scientific or historical research purposes or statistical purposes in accordance with Article 89(1) subject to implementation of the appropriate technical and organisational measures required by this Regulation in order to safeguard the rights and freedoms of the data subject ('storage limitation');

(f) processed in a manner that ensures appropriate security of the personal data, including protection against unauthorised or unlawful processing and against accidental loss, destruction or damage, using appropriate technical or organisational measures ('integrity and confidentiality').

2. The controller shall be responsible for, and be able to demonstrate compliance with, paragraph 1 ('accountability')."[3]

These principles are broadly equivalent to those in the 1998 Data Protection Act:

DPA (1998)	GDPR	Notes
Principle 1 – fair and lawful	Principle (a) – lawfulness, fairness and transparency	See "Lawful basis", below

the execution of criminal penalties, including the safeguarding against and the prevention of threats to public security." - http://eur-lex.europa.eu/legal-content/EN/TXT/PDF/?uri=CELEX:32016L0680&from=EN

Principle 2 – purposes	Principle (b) – purpose limitation	The purposes for processing the data must be clear and documented (including the privacy information for individuals) from the start. The personal data can only be used for a new purpose if either this is compatible with the original purpose, consent is gained, or there is a clear basis in law.
Principle 3 – adequacy	Principle (c) – data minimisation	Processed personal data must be adequate (sufficient to properly fulfil the stated purpose), relevant (has a rational link to that purpose) and limited to what is necessary for that purpose.
Principle 4 – accuracy	Principle (d) – accuracy	All reasonable steps must be taken to ensure that the personal data is not incorrect or misleading as to any matter of fact. This may also require the personal data to be continuously updated, although this depends on what it is being used for. Personal data that is incorrect or misleading must be corrected or erased as soon as possible. NB time-framed data is not subject to the updating requirement[vi]. NB(2) errors may be preserved along with corrections when appropriate, for example a misdiagnosis of a medical condition should continue to be held as part of a patient's medical records even after the diagnosis is corrected, because it is relevant for the purpose of explaining treatment given to the patient, or for other health problems. (see also "Medical opinion", below)

[vi] So it is acceptable to record that I once lived in Hull, but not to record that I still do so.

Principle 5 - retention	Principle (e) – storage limitation	Personal data must not be kept for longer than required. The purposes for keeping it will thus inform the justification for doing so. The ICO recommends implementing a policy that sets standard retention periods, which the NHS has. This means that data should be periodically reviewed and erased or anonymised when no longer required. (See "right to erasure" below). Personal data may be kept for longer if it is for public interest archiving, scientific or historical research, or statistical purposes.
Principle 6 – rights	No principle – separate provisions in Chapter III of the GDPR	
Principle 7 – security	Principle (f) – integrity and confidentiality	Appropriate security measures must be in place to protect the personal data held. Risk analysis, organisational policies and physical and technical measures (such as pseudonymisation and encryption) all form part of this. Additionally, access and availability to personal data must be restored in a timely manner in the event of a physical or technical incident.
Principle 8 – international transfers	No principle – separate provisions in Chapter V of the GDPR	
(no equivalent)	Accountability principle	Controllers and processors are required to take responsibility for what they do with personal data and how they comply with the other principles. They must be able to demonstrate compliance through appropriate measures and records.

Figure 1: DPA/GDPR Comparison Table

The GDPR is, like its predecessors, designed to prevent the misuse of personal data.

In the GDPR, personal data is defined as: *"any information relating to an identified or identifiable natural person ('data subject'); an identifiable natural person is one who can be identified, directly or indirectly, in particular by reference to an identifier such as a name, an identification number, location data, an online identifier or to one or more factors specific to the physical, physiological, genetic, mental, economic, cultural or social identity of that natural person."*[4]

Personal data is therefore information that relates to an individual. That individual must be identified or identifiable either directly or indirectly from one or more identifiers or from factors specific to the individual.

There are also classes of personal data including "special categories of personal data" which have to be processed with a higher level of protection.

These are:

- *"race*
- *ethnic origin*
- *political opinions*
- *religious or philosophical beliefs*
- *trade union membership*
- *genetic data*
- *biometric data (where this is used for identification purposes)*
- *health data*
- *sex life*
- *sexual orientation*
- *information relating to criminal convictions and offences"*[5]

In order to process such data, both a lawful basis (see page 16) must be identified along with a separate condition for processing special category data. These do not have to be linked. There are ten conditions for processing special category data in the GDPR itself, but the Data Protection Act 2018 introduces additional conditions and safeguards. There is detailed guidance at https://ico.org.uk/for-organisations/guide-to-the-general-data-protection-regulation-gdpr/lawful-basis-for-processing/special-category-data/ and https://ico.org.uk/for-organisations/guide-to-the-general-data-protection-regulation-gdpr/lawful-basis-for-processing/criminal-offence-data/ but this level of detail is unnecessary for this book.

The key to personal data is identifiability, i.e. does the information allow an individual to be specifically identified? Whilst a name is probably the most common means of identifying someone, whether any potential identifier (including a name) identifies an individual depends on the context[vii]. The GDPR gives a non-exhaustive list of common identifiers:

- name
- identification number
- location data
- online identifier - these may include information relating to the device that an individual is using, applications, tools or protocols. The use of these may leave traces which, when combined with unique identifiers and other information received by servers, may be used to create profiles of individuals and identify them. They include:
  - internet protocol (IP) addresses
  - cookie identifiers

[vii] As a student, my housemates and I debated who had the most unusual surname. We resolved this by looking up our respective surnames in the Leicestershire telephone directory (which shows how long ago it was). There were no "Ganney"s, so I won, but it does make me very identifiable from only a little information.

- radio frequency identification (RFID) tags
- MAC addresses
- advertising IDs
- pixel tags
- account handles
- device fingerprints[6]

The GDPR also notes that *"one or more factors specific to the physical, physiological, genetic, mental, economic, cultural or social identity of that natural person"*[7] can help to uniquely identify a particular individual as they give information about them[viii]. An individual is also identifiable if you can distinguish that individual from other members of a group[ix].

Indirect identification is possibly the hardest part of "personal data" to ensure compliance with. An individual that cannot be directly identified from the information being processed (for example where all direct identifiers have been removed) may still be identifiable by other means, either from information already held, or information that is needed to be obtained from another source. Also, a third party could use information processed and combine it with other information available to them to identify an individual. The ICO says: *"You must carefully consider all of the means that any party is reasonably likely to use to identify that individual. This is important because you could inadvertently release or disclose information that could be linked with other information and (inappropriately) identify an individual."*[8]

Note "reasonably likely", which is clarified by the ICO: *"Therefore, the fact that there is a very slight hypothetical possibility that someone might be able to reconstruct the data in such a way that the individual is identified is not necessarily sufficient to make the individual identifiable."*[9] All objective factors should be considered, such as:

- the cost and amount of time required for identification
- the available technology at the time of the processing
- likely technological developments

It is important to document this assessment, especially given the third point.

As described earlier, the GDPR defines personal data as *"any information relating to an identified or identifiable natural person ('data subject')"* so we must now consider the meaning of "relates to". Data may be personal data simply because its content is 'obviously about' an individual. However, data may be personal data because it is clearly 'linked to' an individual as it is about his or her activities and it is being processed for the purpose of determining or influencing the way in which that individual is treated. The ICO lists examples of data that 'relates to' an individual because the content of the information is clearly about that individual. These are:

> *"medical history;*
>
> *criminal record;*
>
> *a record of an individual's performance at work; or*
>
> *a record of an individual's sporting achievements."*[10]

Records such as personal bank statements or itemised telephone bills are also personal data as the content of the information is about their activities whilst not being about the individual themselves.

[viii] There is a famous case of the anonymised image (I think MRI) presented at a medical conference to illustrate the speaker's subject. The condition was so rare that other clinicians in the room were able to identify the person from this otherwise anonymised image.

[ix] It is worth noting that CCTV evidence relies on being able to do this.

The key question in determining "personal data" is whether the data can be linked to an individual to provide particular information about that individual. *"If the data is used, or is likely to be used[x], to learn, evaluate, treat in a certain way, make a decision about, or influence the status or behaviour of an individual, then it is personal data."*[11]

Inaccurate information can also be personal data. It may be factually incorrect or be information about a different individual, but the information is still personal data, as it relates to that individual. For example, if a complaint (from a third party) about a ground-floor tenant is wrongly attributed to the top-floor tenant[xi], then it is personal data about both of them, even though it may be inaccurate for one of them. If the complaint specifies that the tenant owns a dog, whereas neither do, then no individual can be identified so it is not personal data.

Note also that an opinion relating to an individual can also be personal data, irrespective of the accuracy of that opinion (but see "medical opinion", page 16).

Finally, data may be personal data when processed by one organisation, but not when processed by another. The ICO gives the example of a photograph of a beach on a sunny day, in which the level of quality means that individuals may be identifiable. If a newspaper publishes it alongside a story about record-breaking temperatures then the journalist has not processed the photograph to learn anything about any of the individuals in it, nor is it likely that the journalist would ever process the photograph for that purpose. Whilst processed by the photographer, the photograph would not be personal data as it is not used to record, learn or decide something about the individuals. However, if an individual in the photograph had taken compassionate leave to attend a (fictional) funeral, then when it is used as disciplinary evidence it has been processed to record, learn or decide something about the individual so it becomes personal data.

There is, of course, a lot more to the GDPR than that. A few other headline points[xii]:

- The penalties for failure:
  - These are significantly stronger than those provided under the DPA. The GDPR describes three levels of non-compliance, each with a band of fines associated with it. For the most serious instances of non-compliance, an organisation can expect a fine of up to 4% of annual global turnover or €20 million, whichever is greater. Processors are legally liable if they are responsible for a breach.
- Rights:
  - There are eight rights for individuals in the GDPR:
    - The right to be informed. (Individuals must be provided with the purposes for processing personal data, the retention periods for that personal data, and who it will be shared with. This set (together with some other information) is called 'privacy information'[xiii]).
    - The right of access. (Individuals have the right to access their personal data, commonly referred to as "subject access". See page 17).
    - The right to rectification. (Individuals have the right to have inaccurate personal data rectified or completed if it is incomplete. This request can be made verbally or in writing, there is one calendar month to respond to a request, but in certain circumstances a request for rectification may be refused).

---

[x] An annoying caveat
[xi] E.g. the complaint specifies "the tenant with a moustache", when both have moustaches.
[xii] There is a very good and very full description on the ICO web site: https://ico.org.uk/for-organisations/guide-to-the-general-data-protection-regulation-gdpr/introduction/
[xiii] This is also known as the "privacy notice". See https://ico.org.uk/for-organisations/guide-to-the-general-data-protection-regulation-gdpr/individual-rights/right-to-be-informed/ for a checklist

- The right to erasure. (Also known as the *Right to Be Forgotten*, individuals can demand under certain circumstances that their personal data be erased by the data controller)[xiv]. See also "medical data", page 17.
- The right to restrict processing. (Individuals have the right (in certain circumstances) to request the restriction or suppression of their personal data. When this applies the personal data may be stored but not used).
- The right to data portability. (Individuals have the right to forward personal data from one data controller to another. The data must be provided in a structured, commonly used machine-readable format[xv].) (See also "Lawful Processing", page 16)
- The right to object. (Individuals have the right to object to the processing of their personal data in certain circumstances. Specifically, they have an absolute right to stop their data being used for direct marketing. In other cases where the right to object applies processing may be allowed to continue if a compelling reason for doing so can be shown).
- Rights in relation to automated decision making and profiling. (Automated individual decision-making (making a decision solely by automated means without any human involvement) and profiling (automated processing of personal data to evaluate certain things about an individual) require additional information to be provided and require explicit consent).

- Compulsory breach reporting:
  - A report of "*a breach of security leading to the accidental or unlawful destruction, loss, alteration, unauthorised disclosure of, or access to, personal data transmitted, stored or otherwise processed*"[xvi][12] must be made to the relevant **Data Protection Regulator** (DPR) and those affected within 72 hours of the breach being identified.
  - On 16th July 2018, UKFast reported that "*since 25th May 2018, there have been 205 reported GDPR breaches registered with the Data Protection Commissioner (DPC). Surprisingly, that's only a third of all reported breaches that have occurred since the GDPR deadline: 918 breaches have been flagged to other agencies*"[13].

- Anonymisation of data subjects:
  - each individual controller or processor should take both technical and organisational measures to ensure personal data be anonymised. In doing so, the GDPR no longer applies: "*The principles of data protection should therefore not apply to anonymous information, namely information which does not relate to an identified or identifiable natural person or to personal data rendered anonymous in such a manner that the data subject is not or no longer identifiable. This Regulation does not therefore concern the processing of such anonymous information, including for statistical or research purposes.*"[14] It should be noted that anonymisation is not always 100% successful as it may still be possible to link the data back to an individual and so is only pseudonymisation (see "Personal Data", below). In addition, when you do anonymise personal data, you are still processing the data at that point, so the GDPR may still apply.

[xiv] If a valid erasure request is received and no exemption applies, then the data must be erased from backup systems as well as live systems. NB Taking data offline may reduce the risk of misuse, but it is still being held. It is permitted though to anonymise the data instead of deleting it, as individuals cannot then be identified from it. There are many technical difficulties in this though, which have been recognised. See https://verasafe.com/blog/article/do-i-need-to-erase-personal-data-from-backup-systems-under-the-gdpr/ for a helpful discussion. This also (in a roundabout way) answers the question as to whether or not you need to keep a record of the deletion (basically, it's a good idea).

[xv] E.g. CSV, XML or JSON.

[xvi] Referred to in the GDPR as a "personal data breach"

- Mandatory **Data Protection Officer** (DPO):
    - all public authorities and organisations where the core business activities include the large-scale processing of personal data must appoint a Data Protection Officer[xvii]. The DPO must be independent, an expert in data protection, adequately resourced, and report to the highest management level.
- Personal data:
    - The pseudonymisation of personal data is of particular interest to those involved with medical imaging, which can fall within the scope of the GDPR depending on how difficult it is to attribute the pseudonym to a particular individual. "Pseudonymisation" is defined as *"the processing of personal data in such a manner that the personal data can no longer be attributed to a specific data subject without the use of additional information, provided that such additional information is kept separately and is subject to technical and organisational measures to ensure that the personal data are not attributed to an identified or identifiable natural person."*[15] It should be noted that pseudonymisation is effectively only a security measure and thus does not change the status of the data as personal data. Recital 26 of the GDPR makes it clear that pseudonymised personal data remains personal data and thus is within the scope of the GDPR.
    - *"The GDPR only applies to information which relates to an identifiable living individual. Information relating to a deceased person does not constitute personal data and therefore is not subject to the GDPR"*.[16]
    - Information concerning a 'legal' rather than a 'natural' person is not personal data. Therefore information about a public authority, a limited company or another legal entity does not constitute personal data and does not fall within the scope of the GDPR. However, the GDPR does apply to personal data relating to individuals acting as sole traders, employees, partners, and company directors wherever they are individually identifiable *and* the information relates to them as an individual rather than as the representative of a legal person[xviii].
    - The ICO's advice is that, if you're unsure if a given piece of information is personal data, then treat it as though it were.
- Lawful processing:
    - For processing to be lawful under the GDPR, a lawful basis must be identified and documented before personal data can be processed (there are six such bases – see page 16). This lawful basis must be determined and documented. Under the GDPR this lawful basis for processing impacts individuals' rights. As mentioned above, if you rely on someone's consent to process their data, they will generally have stronger rights, for example to have their data deleted.
    - *"Consent under the GDPR must be a freely given, specific, informed and unambiguous indication of the individual's wishes"*[17]. There needs to be a clear affirmative action (a positive opt-in – consent cannot be inferred from silence, pre-ticked boxes or inactivity) and must be verifiable. Consent must also be separate from other terms and conditions, and it must be an easy process for consent to be withdrawn. *"Public authorities and employers will need to take particular care to ensure that consent is freely given."*[18] The principles are: *"specific, granular[xix], clear, prominent, opt-in, properly documented and easily withdrawn"*[19]

[xvii] In some cases several organisations can appoint a single DPO between them – especially useful for small organisations
[xviii] *"A name and a corporate email address clearly relates to a particular individual and is therefore personal data. However, the content of any email using those details will not automatically be personal data unless it includes information which reveals something about that individual, or has an impact on them."* – ICO website
[xix] i.e. small – the purpose is to stop blanket opt-ins such as "I want to receive money and spam"

- There are other lawful bases apart from consent, for example where processing is necessary for the purposes of an organisation's legitimate interests, but consent is likely to be the most widely used in healthcare[xx].
- The Lawful Basis will determine which rights are available to individuals. For example, legal obligation does not allow the rights of erasure, portability or objection, whereas consent does not allow objection (but does retain the right to remove consent).
- The six lawful bases are:
  - **Consent**: the individual has given clear consent for the processing of their personal data for a specific purpose[xxi].
  - **Contract**: the processing is necessary for a contract with the individual, or as a preliminary to one.
  - **Legal obligation**: the processing is necessary for compliance with the law.
  - **Vital interests**: the processing is necessary to protect someone's life.
  - **Public task**: the processing is necessary for a task in the public interest or for official functions, and the task or function has a clear basis in law.
  - **Legitimate interests**: the processing is necessary for the legitimate interests of the processor or the legitimate interests of a third party except where such interests are overridden by the interests or fundamental rights and freedoms of the data subject which require protection of personal data, in particular where the data subject is a child.
- More than one legal basis may be required. For example at Liverpool University HR process staff data on a contractual basis, SEE process student data as part of their public task and ERMC Admissions process applicant data based on legitimate interests of recruiting students.

- Unstructured data:
  - The GDPR applies to both automated personal data and to manual filing systems where personal data are accessible according to specific criteria. This could include chronologically ordered sets of manual records containing personal data.
  - The GDPR does not cover information which is not, or is not intended to be, part of a 'filing system'. However, under the DPA 2018 *"unstructured manual information processed only by public authorities constitutes personal data. This includes paper records that are not held as part of a filing system. While such information is personal data under the DPA 2018, it is exempted from most of the principles and obligations in the GDPR and is aimed at ensuring that it is appropriately protected for requests under the Freedom of Information Act 2000."*[20]

- Medical Opinion:
  - A record of an opinion (not just a medical one) is not necessarily inaccurate personal data if it is later proved to be wrong. Opinions are, by their very nature, subjective and not intended to record matters of fact.
  - *"An area of particular sensitivity is medical opinion, where doctors routinely record their opinions about possible diagnoses. It is often impossible to conclude with certainty, perhaps until time has passed or tests have been done, whether a patient is suffering from a particular condition. An initial diagnosis (which is an informed opinion) may prove to be incorrect after more extensive examination or further tests. However, if the patient's records reflect the doctor's diagnosis at the time, the records are not inaccurate, because they accurately reflect that doctor's opinion at a particular time. Moreover, the record of the doctor's initial diagnosis*

[xx] It may be legitimately argued that Vital Interests would be a better one, but is possibly harder to prove quickly, except in A&E.
[xxi] This is the most commonly used basis in healthcare. There is a useful discussion of the issues and techniques in "Ensuring informed consent in an era of information overload" by Andrea Williamson Shemilt in Scope 28:1.

may help those treating the patient later, and in data protection terms is required in order to comply with the 'adequacy' element of the data minimisation principle."[21]

- Medical data:
    - The "right to be forgotten" has rightly raised concern amongst medical professionals. However, Article 17 of the GDPR states that in *certain circumstances* an individual can submit a request to the data controller to have personal information erased or to prevent further processing of that data. This applies when:
        - *The personal data is no longer necessary or relevant in relation to the purpose for which it was original collected*
        - *The individual specifically withdraws consent to processing (and if there is no other justification or legitimate interest for continued processing)*
        - *Personal data has been unlawfully processed, in breach of the GDPR*
        - *The data must be erased in order for a controller to comply with legal obligations (for example, the deletion of certain data after a set period of time)*[22]
    - In conjunction with this, those collecting health data will normally choose to rely on consent. However, an organisation does not have to rely on consent and can collect and use health data if the processing is necessary for the purposes of preventive or occupational medicine, medical diagnosis, provision of health or social care or treatment, management of health or social care systems and services, under a contract with a health professional or another person subject to professional secrecy under law (the 'medical care' ground). Additionally, consent is not required if the processing is necessary in the public interest for public health reasons (the 'public health' ground), or if the organisation can argue that the processing is necessary for scientific research. The "public health ground" is "processing is necessary for reasons of public interest in the area of public health, such as protecting against serious cross-border threats to health or ensuring high standards of quality and safety of health care and of medicinal products or medical devices, on the basis of Union or Member State law which provides for suitable and specific measures to safeguard the rights and freedoms of the data subject, in particular professional secrecy;
    - Thus, it may be argued, the "right to be forgotten" does NOT apply to medical data.

The GDPR, like the DPA before it, gives individuals the right to access their personal data. This is known as a "subject access request". Individuals can make a subject access request verbally or in writing, and the organisation has one month[xxii] in which to respond to a request. A fee to deal with this request cannot be charged in most circumstances[xxiii].

Individuals have the right to obtain confirmation that their personal data is being processed, a copy of their personal data and other supplementary information. This includes:

- the purposes of processing
- the categories of personal data concerned
- the recipients or categories of recipient the personal data is disclosed to
- the retention period for storing the personal data or, where this is not possible, the criteria for determining how long it will be stored
- the existence of their right to request rectification, erasure or restriction or to object to such processing

---

[xxii] This can be extended by a further two months if the request is complex or if several requests have been received from the individual. The individual must be informed within one month of receiving their request and given an explanation as to why the extension is necessary.

[xxiii] A "reasonable fee" for the administrative costs of complying with the request may be charged where the request is manifestly unfounded or excessive. Also, if an individual requests further copies of their data following a request. The fee must be based on the administrative costs of providing further copies.

- the right to lodge a complaint with the ICO or another supervisory authority
- information about the source of the data, where it was not obtained directly from the individual
- the existence of automated decision-making (including profiling)
- the safeguards provided if personal data is transferred to a third country or international organisation.

Much of this information may already be provided in the organisation's privacy notice. The GDPR includes a best practice recommendation that, where possible, organisations should be able to provide remote access to a secure self-service system which would provide the individual with direct access to his or her information[xxiv]. The information must be capable of being understood by the average person,[xxv] which means that codes (e.g. Ethnic Origin) must be transcribed.

There are special considerations when dealing with children's data. The ICO lists 11, including:

- Children may be less aware of the risks involved.
- Consent is one possible lawful basis for processing a child's personal data, but it is not the only option. In the UK only children aged 13 or over are able provide their own consent.
- Decisions based solely on automated processing about children cannot be made if this will have a legal or similarly significant effect on them.
- Privacy notices for children need to be clear so that they can understand what will happen to their personal data, and what rights they have.
- Children have the same rights as adults over their personal data, including the rights to access, clarify, object and erasure. An individual's right to erasure is particularly relevant if they gave their consent to processing when they were a child.[xxvi]

Of course, all these protections only apply to data within the EU, so the GDPR also restricts the transfer of personal data outside of the EU, unless the rights of the individuals in respect of their personal data is protected in another way, or one of a limited number of exceptions applies.

First overview on the implementation of the GDPR
The **European Data Protection Board** (EDPB) published a one year on review[23], the major findings of which were:

- The national **Supervisory Authorities** (SAs) reported a total of 206,326 cases within the first year of GDPR's implementation. All of these cases pertained to one of three subject matters. Close to half (94,622) dealt with complaints, while 64,684 of those reports concerned data breach notifications. The remaining cases focused on "other" issues.
- Within that time period, authorities closed just over half (52%) of those cases.
- Under the GDPR SAs have different types of corrective powers which they can use with an offending data processor or controller. These include: issuing warnings and reprimands, ordering that the entity bring its operations into compliance with the regulation and imposing fines. From 25 May 2018 to 21 May 2019, the 31 SAs imposed a total of €55,955,871 in administrative fines[xxvii].
- There are two tiers of fines:
  - Tier 1 (with a cap of 2% of global turnover or €10 million, whichever is higher) including:
    - Failure to appoint an independent and fully supported DPO.
    - Failure to complete a **Data Protection Impact Assessment** (DPIA) for high-risk activities.
    - Failure to notify the supervisory authority of a data breach within 72 hours.

[xxiv] Recital 63

[xxv] Note "average person" not necessarily the person making the request.

[xxvi] Guidance is available at https://ico.org.uk/for-organisations/guide-to-the-general-data-protection-regulation-gdpr/children-and-the-gdpr/what-rights-do-children-have/

[xxvii] In October 2020, the ICO fined British Airways £20m for a data breach affecting more than 400,000 customers.

- Failure to notify a data subject of a data breach without undue delay.
  - o Tier 2 (with a cap of 4% of global turnover or €20 million, whichever is higher) including:
    - Failure to adhere to the six data protection principles.
    - Failure to demonstrate data subject consent.
    - Failure to comply with data subject access requests.
    - Failure to comply with the right to erasure and data portability requirements.
    - Failure to ensure adequate legal mechanisms for data transfer to countries outside the European Economic Area.

The Freedom of Information Act 2000

The FOI is a UK law (although there are many similar laws elsewhere, especially in Europe) that describes the rights of groups and individuals to request information and the obligations of the organisation to respond to such requests. All public authorities in England, Northern Ireland and Wales and those which are UK-wide have a legal obligation to provide information through an approved publication scheme and in response to requests. Scotland has a similar Act, the Freedom of Information (Scotland) Act 2002 which is regulated by the Scottish Information Commissioner's Office.

Under the FOI Act[xxviii], a member of the public has the right to ask for any information they think a public authority may hold. The right only covers recorded information which includes information held on computers, in emails and in printed or handwritten documents as well as images, video and audio recordings.

A request is made directly to the relevant authority, in writing. The request may be in the form of a question and must contain the requester's real name and a contact address for the reply.

The request must be responded to within 20 working days. This response can take one of the following forms:

- *provide the information requested;*
- *respond that the authority doesn't have the information;*
- *respond that another authority holds the information.* The authority may (but does not have to) transfer the request;
- *respond that the information is available and can be provided for a fee* (but there are rules surrounding this);
- *refuse to provide the information,* and explain why; or,
- *respond that more time is required to consider the public interest in disclosing or withholding the information,* and state when a response should be expected. This should not be later than 40 working days after the date of the request. The time limit can only be extended in certain circumstances, and an explanation as to why the information may be exempt must be provided.

The request may be refused for the following reasons:

- *It will cost too much to provide.* The limit is currently set at £600 for any government department, Houses of Parliament, Northern Ireland Assembly, National Assembly for Wales, Welsh Assembly Government and armed forces and £450 for any other public bodies. This is interpreted as being 24 and 18 hours' effort, respectively. (i.e. about two and a half days' work for the NHS).
- *The request is vexatious or repeated.*
- *The information is exempt from disclosure under one of the exemptions in the Act.* There are 23 exemptions in the Act, broadly divided into three categories:
  - Those that apply to a whole category (or class) of information, for example, information about investigations and proceedings conducted by public authorities, court records and trade secrets.

---

xxviii Essentially an addenda to the Public Records Act, which itself had to be modified to take account of the FOI

- Those that are subject to a 'prejudice' test, where disclosure would, or would be likely to, prejudice for example the interests of the United Kingdom abroad, the prevention or detection of crime or the activity or interest described in the exemption.
- Requests that should be dealt with under the DPA either as a subject access request, or releasing the information would contravene the DPA (e.g. where the FOI request is about a third party).
- It is worth noting that a request may not be refused because part of a document that would have to be provided is exempt. In this case, a redacted version of the document with the exempt information removed must be provided.

There are some very good examples on the ICO web site[24] of how to interpret these exclusions.

This leads to the question of anonymised data, where all person-identifiable information has been removed. For example, a request to provide an anonymised MRI image. This would seem to satisfy the requirements of a FOI request, but is not one of the purposes for which the data was collected, so is exempt via the DPA (unless, of course, it was included in the consent form). We'll look at how metadata is attached to medical images in chapter 5.

Whilst we are considering anonymised data, it is worth mentioning synonymisation or pseudonymisation: that is, the process of removing all patient-identifiable data (for example, from a **Digital Imaging and Communications in Medicine** (DICOM) header) and replacing it with another identifier, for example a research number, so that all data relating to that study can be kept together, without having to reference the patient.

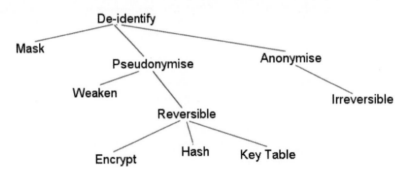

Figure 2: Different Kinds of De-identification

There are several kinds of de-identification as illustrated in Figure 2. The key questions in determining the most appropriate kind of de-identification are:

1. Who are you keeping the identity from?
2. Where could a motivated attacker find the identity?

Note that anonymisation is irreversible, whereas pseudonymisation is not. For imaging data, true anonymisation may require the removal of so much detail that the image is no longer clinically useful. It may, therefore, not be possible to do this and pseudonymisation must be used. A DICOM confidentiality profile will list all the attributes that require attention (and what should be done with them).

The Caldicott Committee
The Caldicott Committee was established in 1997, to review the flow of patient-identifiable information around and out of the NHS. It was chaired by Dame Fiona Caldicott (hence the name) who was Chief Medical Officer for England at the time. Its work resulted in an instruction to all NHS Chief Executives to appoint Caldicott Guardians by the end of March 1999.

The Caldicott Guardian is a senior member of staff whose role is to:

- *establish the highest practical standards for handling patient information;*
- *produce a year on year improvement plan for ensuring patient confidentiality;*
- *monitor yearly improvement against the improvement plan;*
- *agree and review protocols governing the protection and use of patient identifiable information;*
- *agree and review protocols governing the disclosure of patient information;*
- *develop the Trust security and confidentiality policy.*

The implication of this is that approval of the Caldicott Guardian must be gained for all new flows of patient data except data to be used for research purposes[xxix]. The decision of the Caldicott Guardian is final and may not be challenged.

On the international scene information is protected through the ISO 27000 family of standards. In particular, ISO 27799: 2008 'Health Informatics - Information Security Management in Health using IEC / ISO 20002' covers the principles described, together with the provision of accredited Information Security Management Systems.

In summarising the principles surrounding the proper protection of data the NHS Information Strategy adopted the acronym CIA (**Confidentiality, Integrity and Access**). Whilst data must be kept confidential and its integrity is paramount; it must also be readily accessible to those who need it.

Caldicott2

The Caldicott2 Review Panel in 2013 revised the Caldicott Principles and recommended that they should be adopted and promulgated throughout the health and social care system. The Government accepted this recommendation in their response to the Caldicott2 Review ("To share or not to share"). Dame Fiona Caldicott became the **National Data Guardian** for Health and Care (NDG) in 2015. One of the things that she did while in this role was in 2017 when she admonished The Royal free Hospital for allowing Google's DeepMind AI system free access to all of its patient data, when the agreement was only for a kidney injury alert system.

The revised principles (Revised September 2013) are[25]:

Principle 1. Justify the purpose(s) for using confidential information
Every proposed use or transfer of personal confidential data within or from an organisation should be clearly defined, scrutinised and documented, with continuing uses regularly reviewed, by an appropriate guardian.

Principle 2. Don't use personal confidential data unless it is absolutely necessary
Personal confidential data items should not be included unless it is essential for the specified purpose(s) of that flow. The need for patients to be identified should be considered at each stage of satisfying the purpose(s).

Principle 3. Use the minimum necessary personal confidential data
Where use of personal confidential data is considered to be essential, the inclusion of each individual item of data should be considered and justified so that the minimum amount of personal confidential data is transferred or accessible as is necessary for a given function to be carried out.

Principle 4. Access to personal confidential data should be on a strict need-to-know basis
Only those individuals who need access to personal confidential data should have access to it, and they should only have access to the data items that they need to see. This may mean introducing access controls or splitting data flows where one data flow is used for several purposes.

[xxix] It was not so in the original terms of reference for the review and was assumed to be covered by the ethics committee instead. Caldicott2 acknowledges the importance of data being available for research.

Principle 5. Everyone with access to personal confidential data should be aware of their responsibilities
Action should be taken to ensure that those handling personal confidential data - both clinical and non-clinical staff - are made fully aware of their responsibilities and obligations to respect patient confidentiality.

Principle 6. Comply with the law
Every use of personal confidential data must be lawful. Someone in each organisation handling personal confidential data should be responsible for ensuring that the organisation complies with legal requirements.

Principle 7. The duty to share information can be as important as the duty to protect patient confidentiality
Health and social care professionals should have the confidence to share information in the best interests of their patients within the framework set out by these principles. They should be supported by the policies of their employers, regulators and professional bodies.

Information Commissioner and Clinical Information Officer
The **Information Commissioner's Office** (ICO) is *"The UK's independent authority set up to uphold information rights in the public interest, promoting openness by public bodies and data privacy for individuals"*[26]. A healthcare organisation which handles personal information may need to register with the ICO as a data controller. Notification is a statutory requirement and every organisation that processes personal information must notify the ICO, unless they are exempt. Failure to notify is a criminal offence. If in doubt, there is plenty of advice on their web site.

The CIO is the **Clinical Information Officer** and is more commonly referred to as a CCIO (Chief CIO). Each Trust should have one (although it's not mandatory) and he or she should report to the Chief Exec, being part of the Executive Board. Generally this role will be filled by a senior clinician (but does not need to be). Broadly, the role of the CCIO is required to support the strategic aims of the Hospital taking particular responsibility for:

- *Ensuring clinical adoption and engagement in use of technology*
- *Driving continuous clinical process improvement focused on patient outcomes and efficiency*
- *Developing clinical Information that supports and enhances organisational reform*

Chapter 2 - NHS strategy for ICT in Healthcare

The NHS mandate published by the Department of Health in 2012, said: "*In a digital age, it is crucial that the NHS not only operates at the limits of medical science, but also increasingly at the forefront of new technologies. The (National Commissioning) Board's[i] objective is to achieve a significant increase in the use of technology to help people manage their health and care.*"

There is no single strategy, but it has been left to Trusts to develop their own (e.g. Royal Wolverhampton[27]). This might be achieved through:

- Standardisation of care – e.g. electronic care pathways, electronic clinical decision support systems
- Mobile computing devices
- Tele-medicine and Tele-health
- Flexible access: web sites, booking systems, direct communication with care teams
- Co-ordinated care across providers
- Convergence of information, data and communication technologies

There are some (but not as many as you might think) NHS standards for ICT. Examples are:

- DICOM and **Health Language 7** (HL7) (see pages 45 and 54)
- Snomed[28]
- The code of conduct for data-driven health and care technology[29]

In January 2019, the NHS launched its "Long Term Plan", which "*sets out our ambitions for improvement over the next decade, following the five year funding settlement announced by the government in July 2018*".[30] This plan contains a chapter entitled "Digitally-enabled primary and outpatient care will go mainstream across the NHS" which sets out plans for interoperability of data and systems, the use of **Artificial Intelligence** (AI) and more convenient ways of accessing advice and care (digital appointments, prescriptions and consultations – both remote video and virtual). The plan notes that this is not a huge paradigm shift, but a continuation of the current direction of travel – it gives case studies to back up its claims that these things are both possible and necessary, noting that "*The NHS is a hotbed of innovation and technological revolution in clinical practice*"[31] and citing the **Electronic Prescription Service** (EPS) which it quotes as being used in 93% of England's 7,300 GP practices, with more than 67% of their prescriptions delivered via EPS. The plan claims that this has improved patient experience and saved the NHS £136 million in the three years from 2013 to 2016[ii].

The plan is not shy of the challenge and does outline some of the obstacles to be overcome. The chapter on digital care concludes with the environment and infrastructure required for the desired innovation to thrive, to be enabled by:

- "*creating a secure and capable digitally literate workforce;*
- *requiring every technology supplier to the NHS to comply with published open standards to enable interoperability and continual improvement;*
- *making solutions that are commissioned and developed by the NHS available as 'open source' to the developer community so that they can build on and enhance them to meet the evolving needs of the NHS and our patients;*
- *ensuring that LHCR[iii] data platforms provide open and free APIs for developers to create new solutions that can compete with and, where appropriate, replace the traditional solutions used by the NHS;*

---

[i] NHS England's legal name is the National Health Service Commissioning Board
[ii] Very difficult to measure empirically, but believable.
[iii] Local Health and Care Record

- *making available a set of central capabilities that are rapidly deployable and can be used as the basis for future local innovation and development, such as the NHS Login or the national record locator service."[32]*

Underpinning and predating the plan, there are two compulsory **Data Coordination Board** (DCB) standards that are mandatory under the Health and Social Care Act 2012. DCB0129[iv] describes the risk management processes required to minimise risks to patient safety with respect to the manufacture of health software products either as new systems or as changes to existing systems. DCB0160[v] is similar, describing the deployment of such products. Thus many healthcare sites need to comply with DCB0129 and all with DCB0160. A fully populated hazard log may be used to demonstrate compliance, and compliance with DCB0160 will encompass compliance with IEC 80001-1 – both of these topics will be covered later.

In June 2022 the Department of Health and Social Care published a new data strategy, "Data saves lives: reshaping health and social care with data" which aims to improve data health standards. It contains a range of concrete commitments, which includes:

- *"Investing in secure data environments to power life-saving research and treatments.*
- *Using technology to allow staff to spend more quality time with patients.*
- *Giving people better access to their own data through shared care records and the NHS App."[33]*

The seven principles of the strategy are:

- *"Improving trust in the health and care system's use of data.*
- *Giving health and care professionals the information they need to provide the best care.*
- *Improving data for adult social care.*
- *Supporting local decision-makers with data.*
- *Empowering researchers with the data they need to develop life-changing treatments and diagnostics.*
- *Working with partners to develop innovations that improve health and care.*
- *Developing the right technical infrastructure."[34]*

[iv] Clinical Risk Management: its Application in the Manufacture of Health IT Systems
[v] Clinical Risk Management: its Application in the Deployment and Use of Health IT Systems

Chapter 3 – Operational Management Requirements

The topics encompassed by this title are:

- Methods of protecting the security of the **Picture Archiving and Communications System** (PACS), patient information systems and system security clearances.
- Operational procedures in the various imaging modalities and key imaging requirements.
- Operations of major components of computers, including hardware, software, computer topologies and networks.
- Implications of upgrades (hardware and software).
- Operational management requirements for critical systems.

We will cover computer hardware, software and networking here and consider the other topics in chapters 6 and 10.

Networking and the network environment

Whilst a computer on its own is a powerful device, the possibilities and the power increase greatly when such devices are linked together to form a network.

The minimum number of devices in a network is 2[i]. The maximum number depends on the addressing method: standard IP addresses allow for 4,294,967,296[ii] (256^4) but there are many ways to extend this, as we shall see.

In a hospital environment, devices are usually connected physically – i.e. with a cable. This improves reliability as well as giving larger bandwidth and higher speed. There are multiple ways of connecting devices, but the simplest is via a hub, which is essentially a connection box where all incoming signals are sent to all connected devices.

The Network Packet

All networking is described in terms of packets. A network packet is a formatted unit of data carried by a packet-switched network. Computer communications links that do not support packets, such as traditional point-to-point telecommunications links, simply transmit data as a bit stream.

A packet consists of control information and user data, which is also known as the payload. Control information provides data for delivering the payload, for example: source and destination network addresses, error detection codes, and sequencing information. Typically, control information is found in packet headers and trailers.

Different communication protocols use different conventions for distinguishing between the elements and for formatting the data. For example, in Point-to-Point Protocol, the packet is formatted in 8-bit bytes, and special characters are used to delimit the different elements. Other protocols like Ethernet establish the start of the header and data elements by their location relative to the start of the packet. Some protocols format the information at bit level instead of at byte level.

A good analogy is to consider a packet to be like a letter: the header is like the envelope, and the data area is whatever the person puts inside the envelope.

In the seven-layer OSI (**Open Systems Interconnection**) model of computer networking (see page 47 for a full description, but for now we need only consider that the higher the layer number, the more sophisticated the model), "packet" strictly refers to a data unit at layer 3, the Network Layer. The correct term for a data unit at Layer 2, the Data Link Layer, is a frame, and at Layer 4, the Transport Layer, the correct term is a segment or datagram. For the case of TCP/IP (**Transmission Control Protocol/Internet Protocol**) communication over Ethernet, a TCP segment is carried in one or more IP packets, which are each carried in one or more Ethernet frames.

---

[i] Otherwise you're talking to yourself – this figure excludes virtual networking
[ii] It seems like a large number, but with a world population running at 7 billion, that's only 0.5 IP addresses each.

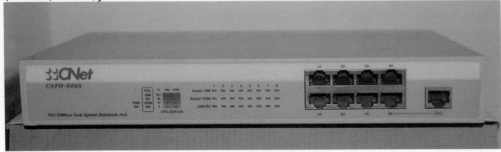

Figure 3: A Network Hub[35]

A hub is a simple connection box operating at the Physical Layer (layer 1) of the OSI model (see page 47). Like a transport hub, it's where everything comes together. Unlike a transport hub, though, whatever comes in on one connection goes out on all other connections. It's up to the receiver to decide whether or not the message is for them. Hubs therefore work well for small networks, but get messy and slow down for larger ones. It is therefore often common to find them in small networks (e.g. at home) or in sub-networks (e.g. in an office).

Figure 4: A Network Switch[36]

A switch is a device that filters and forwards packets between **Local Area Network** (LAN) segments. Switches operate at the data link layer (layer 2) and sometimes the network layer (layer 3 – a higher layer and therefore more sophisticated than a hub) of the OSI Reference Model and therefore support any packet protocol. LANs that use switches to join segments are called switched LANs or, in the case of Ethernet networks, switched Ethernet LANs (as you might expect). Both hubs and switches may be referred to as "bridges".

Figure 5: A Network Router[37]

A router forwards data packets along networks. A router is connected to at least two networks and is located at a gateway, the place where two or more networks connect. Routers use headers and forwarding tables to determine the best path for forwarding the packets, and they use protocols such as **Internet Control Message Protocol** (ICMP) to communicate with each other and configure the best route between any two hosts.

A large network will therefore contain all 3 of these types of devices and we will now compare them.

Routers have generally increased in sophistication, combining the features and functionality of a router and switch/hub into a single unit (and may contain a basic **Domain Name Service** (DNS)).

The functions of a router, hub and a switch are all quite different from one another, even if at times they are all integrated into a single device. We will start with the hub and the switch since these two devices have similar roles within the network.

Both the switch and the hub serve as central connections for all of the network equipment and handle a data type known as frames. Frames carry data and when one is received, it is amplified and then transmitted on to the port of the destination device. The big difference between these two devices is in the method in which frames are being delivered.

In a hub, a frame is passed along or "broadcast" to every one of its ports. It doesn't matter that the frame may be only destined for one port as the hub has no way of distinguishing which port a frame should be sent to. Passing it along to every port ensures that it will reach its intended destination. This places a lot of traffic on the network and can lead to poor network response times.

Additionally, a 10/100Mbps[iii] hub must share its bandwidth across each and every one of its ports. So when only one device is broadcasting, it will have access to the maximum available bandwidth. If, however, multiple devices are broadcasting, then that bandwidth will need to be divided among all of those systems, which will degrade performance.

A switch, however, keeps a record of the **Media Access Control** (MAC) addresses of all the devices connected to it. With this information, a switch can identify which system is sitting on which port. So when a frame is received, it knows exactly which port to send it to, without significantly increasing network response times. And, unlike a hub, a 10/100Mbps switch will allocate a full 10/100Mbps to each of its ports. So regardless of the number of devices transmitting, users will always have access to the maximum amount of bandwidth. For these reasons a switch is considered to be a much better choice than a hub in many situations.

Routers are completely different devices. Where a hub or switch is concerned with transmitting frames, a router's job, as its name implies, is to route packets to other networks until that packet ultimately reaches its destination. One of the key features of a packet is that it not only contains data, but the destination address of where it's going.

A router is typically connected to at least two networks, commonly two LANs or **Wide Area Networks** (WANs) or a LAN and its **Internet Service Provider** (ISP)'s network. For example, a home network and the Internet.

Routers might have a single WAN port and a single LAN port and are designed to connect an existing LAN hub or switch to a WAN. Ethernet switches and hubs can be connected to a router with multiple PC ports to expand a LAN. Some routers have USB ports, and more commonly, wireless access points built into them.

Besides the inherent protection features provided by the **Network Address Translation** (NAT), many routers will also have a built-in, configurable, hardware-based firewall. Firewall capabilities can range from the very basic to quite sophisticated devices. Among the capabilities found on leading routers are those that permit configuring **Transmission Control Protocol/User Datagram Protocol** (TCP/UDP) ports for games, chat services, and the like, on the LAN behind the firewall. (See page 35 for a further description of firewalls).

[iii] bps = **bits per second**

So, in summary, a hub glues together an Ethernet network segment, a switch can connect multiple Ethernet segments more efficiently and a router can do those functions plus route TCP/IP packets between multiple LANs and/or WANs; and much more.

It may seem that routers are therefore significantly better than bridges for connecting parts of a network together. However, bridges pass all network traffic whereas routers only handle directed traffic. Network wide broadcasts are inherently local in scope which means that they are passed along by hubs and switches, but not by routers. "*This is crucial, otherwise the global Internet would be swamped with "broadcasts" and the world would end*".[38] The Windows "Network Neighborhood[iv]" file and printer browsing depends upon network broadcasts to allow locally connected machines to find each other on the LAN – these broadcasts therefore stop at the router, so placing a shared printer on the wrong side of a router is not only poor design, it also leads to significant user frustration.

Network Topologies
The topology of the network can be thought of as its shape. Not its physical shape, but its logical one: much like the London Underground map shows how stations connect, not where they are. The five basic topologies are bus, ring, star, tree and mesh, which we will now examine.

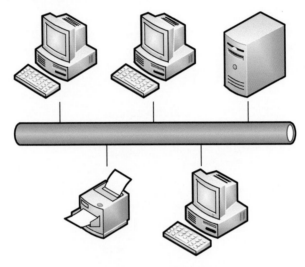

Figure 6: Bus Topology

Bus networks use a common backbone to connect all devices. A single cable, the backbone, functions as a shared communication medium that devices attach or tap into with an interface connector. A device wanting to communicate with another device on the network sends a broadcast message onto the wire that all other devices see, but only the intended recipient actually accepts and processes it.

Ethernet bus topologies are relatively easy to install and don't require much cabling compared to the alternatives. However, bus networks work best with a limited number of devices. If more than a few dozen computers are added to a network bus, performance problems will be the likely result. In addition, if the backbone cable fails, the entire network effectively becomes unusable.

---

iv Updated to "My Network Places" from Windows 7 onwards

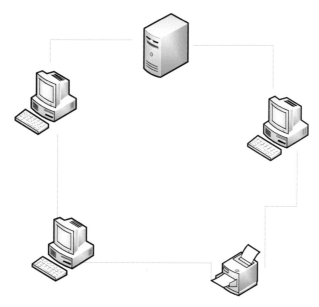

Figure 7: Ring Topology

In a ring network, every device has exactly two neighbours for communication purposes. All messages travel through a ring in the same direction (either "clockwise" or "anticlockwise"). A failure in any cable or device breaks the loop and can take down the entire network.

To implement a ring network, we would typically use FDDI[v], SONET[vi], or Token Ring technology[vii].

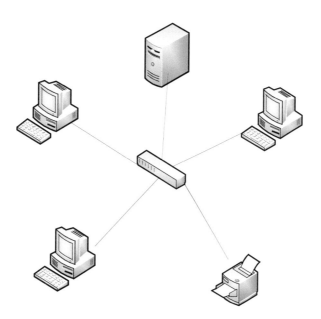

Figure 8: Star Topology

---

[v] **Fibre Distributed Data Interface** – a set of ANSI and ISO standards for data transmission on fibre optic lines in a LAN that can extend in range up to 200 km (124 miles).

[vi] **Synchronous Optical Network** – the American National Standards Institute standard for synchronous data transmission on optical media.

[vii] In a token ring, a "token" is passed around the network. The device holding the "token" is permitted to transmit – nothing else is. If a device has nothing to transmit, it passes the token on.

Most small (e.g. home) networks use the star topology. A star network features a central connection point called a "hub node" that may be a network hub, switch or (more likely) a router. Devices typically connect to the hub with **Unshielded Twisted Pair** (UTP) Ethernet.

Compared to the bus topology, a star network generally requires more cable, but a failure in any star network cable will only take down one computer's network access and not the entire LAN. (If the hub fails, however, the entire network also fails.)

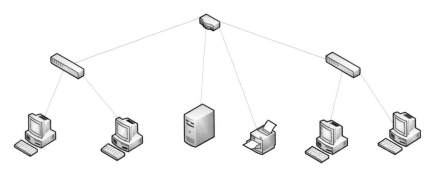

Figure 9: Tree Topology

Tree topologies integrate multiple star topologies together onto a bus. In its simplest form, only hub devices connect directly to the tree bus, and each hub functions as the root of a tree of devices. This bus/star hybrid approach supports future expandability of the network much better than a bus (which is limited in the number of devices due to the broadcast traffic it generates) or a star (which is limited by the number of hub connection points) alone.

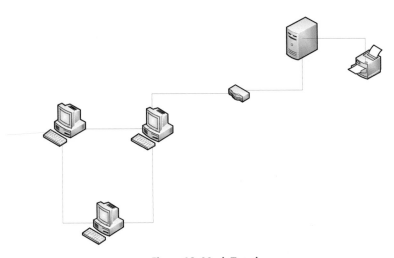

Figure 10: Mesh Topology

Mesh topologies involve the concept of routes. Unlike each of the previous topologies, messages sent on a mesh network can take any of several possible paths from source to destination. (Recall that even in a ring, although two cable paths exist, messages can only travel in one direction.) Some WANs, most notably the Internet, employ mesh routing, specifically for the resilience that it brings.

A mesh network in which every device connects to every other is called a full mesh. As shown in the illustration above, partial mesh networks also exist in which some devices connect only indirectly to others.

IP addressing and DNS

People like to communicate using names. You won't hear goalkeepers call out "1" as they rush off their line to flap hopelessly at an overhead ball, instead of "keeper". Likewise, referring to one's spouse as "number 2" isn't going to go down well. Therefore we call our devices "Linac B PC", "Endoscopy control" and so on.

Computers prefer numbers. When they're communicating, they require unique numbers. Therefore they use **Internet Protocol** (IP) addresses. An IP version 4 address is formed of 4 groups of digits, separated by dots[viii]. Each group of digits can range in value from 0 to 255 – 256[ix] unique numbers. The combination of these 4 groups should uniquely identify the device on the network. If it's not unique then chaos will ensue.

Of course, we still like to call our devices by names, so a network service called a DNS is usually available to translate "LinacA" into 123.45.67.89 so that the command "ping LinacA[x]" can be issued and a reply can come from 123.45.67.89 without the user having to know the IP address of LinacA.

IP mask

The four-byte IP address allows us to perform grouping. A set of devices may be given addresses in the same range with only the final one or two bytes being different. Given that we have a DNS to do the translation and can therefore give our devices sensible names this may seem unnecessary, but it does allow us to segregate our network using masking.

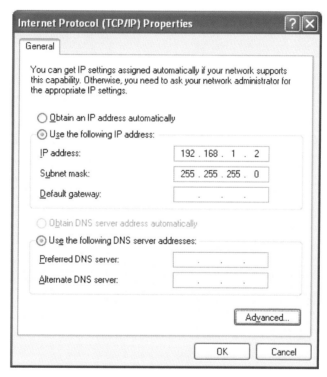

Figure 11: An IP Setup Dialog from Windows XP

An IP mask of 255.255.255.0 allows us to separate out the network prefix and the host number using bitwise AND.

AND does what it sounds like it should: something is true if both the first part AND the second part are true. If either part is false, the result is false. We write this in a truth table as:

[viii] IPv6 also exists, but is not widespread (yet), but does allow 2^{96} addresses

[ix] Due to binary: 256 is 2^8 so each group of digits is composed of 8 bits

[x] A command that sends an "are you there" message.

Input 1	Input 2	Output
FALSE	FALSE	FALSE
FALSE	TRUE	FALSE
TRUE	FALSE	FALSE
TRUE	TRUE	TRUE

Figure 12: Truth Table for the AND Operator

It is common to take "1" to mean TRUE and "0" to mean FALSE, rendering our table as:

Input 1	Input 2	Output
0	0	0
0	1	0
1	0	0
1	1	1

Figure 13: Truth Table for AND using Binary Values

For example, 5 AND 3 can be written as 101 AND 011 in binary form, so using the table above to compare them bit by bit, the result is 001, or simply 1 in decimal notation.

In the example in Figure 11 the network address is 192.168.1 and the host number is 2[xi]. Networks can be further divided to produce smaller subnets by putting more bits into the mask. For example a mask of 255.255.255.192 leaves this example with the same host number, but a host number previously of 130 would now be rendered as 2[xii].

The modern way of specifying a network mask is to specify the number of bits in it, as masks are always 1s to the left and 0s to the right and no intermingling. Thus 192.168.1.2, netmask 255.255.255.0 is written as 192.168.1.2/24 as there are 24 1s in the netmask. This is known as **Classless Inter-Domain Routing** (CIDR) notation.

It is this subnetting that allows us to write simple router rules as they can be produced for groups of IPs instead of for each one individually. By grouping similar devices together, the router rules can be such as 138.0.5.* rather than 100 separate IP addresses.

Ports

An IP address may contain a port number. This is a software port, not to be confused with the hardware ports we discussed earlier in the hardware section. One such example is:

> http://10.5.90.148:71

Here the IP address is 10.5.90.148 and the port number is 71. The port number is a 16-bit integer so can range from 0 to 65535 and it identifies a specific process to which the network message is to be forwarded when it arrives at a server. For TCP and UDP, the port number is put in the header appended to the message unit. This port number is passed logically between client and server transport layers and physically between the transport layer and the IP layer and forwarded on.

Some common port numbers[xiii] are[39]:

> 20: **File Transfer Protocol** (FTP) Data Transfer

> 21: File Transfer Protocol (FTP) Command Control

[xi] n AND 255 = n as 255 = 11111111_2; n AND 0 = 0, so 255.255.255 uses the first three bytes to form the network address, leaving the remainder as the host number.

[xii] As 130 AND 192 = 2

[xiii] The lowest-numbered 1024 are known as the "well-known port numbers" – there is a fuller list at http://packetlife.net/media/library/23/common_ports.pdf

22: **Secure Shell** (SSH) Secure Login

23: Telnet remote login service, unencrypted text messages

25: **Simple Mail Transfer Protocol** (SMTP) E-mail routing

53: Domain Name System (DNS) service

80: **Hypertext Transfer Protocol** (HTTP) used in the World Wide Web

110: **Post Office Protocol** (POP3)

119: **Network News Transfer Protocol** (NNTP)

123: **Network Time Protocol** (NTP)

143: **Internet Message Access Protocol** (IMAP) Management of digital mail

161: **Simple Network Management Protocol** (SNMP)

194: **Internet Relay Chat** (IRC)

443: **HTTP Secure** (HTTPS) HTTP over TLS/SSL[xiv]

Static, dynamic and reserved IPs

There are 3 main ways of giving a device an IP address. Firstly, and most simply, is static. This is where the 4-byte number is given to that device and that device only (see Figure 11 where this is the case).

The second is dynamic. This is where a device requests an IP address from the DHCP[xv] controller and is provided with the next spare one. This system works well with hot-spots and networks where there are more devices than IP addresses, but never has all the devices switched on at once. It's also very useful in networks where the number of devices changes frequently (e.g. a hospital network): no-one has to keep note of the addresses issued so far and no-one has to check whether a device has been decommissioned. Administratively it's the simplest method, but it too has drawbacks.

The main drawback is that some protocols have to communicate via fixed IP addresses. DICOM is one such (although later devices can often take the device name, many can't). One solution to this is to run a mixed addressing network, with some static IPs (usually in the same range so they can be easily administered) and the rest dynamic. One other solution is to use reserved IPs – in this case it is again all controlled by the DHCP controller (often part of the DNS), but when a device requests an IP it is always served the same one, which has been reserved for it. That way the network runs in dynamic mode but the needs of static addressing are met.

The problem with mixed addressing is that it requires more administration, especially to ensure that the fixed range and the static range do not overlap. On initial set-up this may be achieved by, for example, allocating addresses 0-100 to be static and addresses 101-127 to be dynamic. Problems may arise if the static range needs to be increased and the DHCP cluster (as a large organisation will have more than one DHCP server) is still dynamically issuing some IPs that ought to be static.

[xiv] Both TLS (Transport Layer Security) and SSL (Secure Socket Layers) are protocols that assist to securely authenticate and transport data on the Internet. Both connect to https. SSL was deprecated in 2015 and replaced by TLS, although phrases such as "SSL certificate" still exist and are valid. TLS can thus be thought of as "the latest version of SSL".
[xv] Dynamic Host Configuration Protocol

2 Devices with the same IP address

Locally this is impossible, but globally not so. If a device's IP address is only visible up to the router, then it is not visible beyond it (e.g. on the internet) and therefore another device on the other side of the router can have exactly the same IP address and they will never conflict.

This is achieved by address translation: the router uses one set of addresses on one side (e.g. the hospital network) and another on the other side (e.g. the internet), which it translates between dynamically. In that way, the hospital can continue to grow its IP network without worrying that it will clash with another one. The only real problems arise if more Internet addresses are required than the hospital owns, in which case it buys more (although this end is often sorted out by the ISP).

NAT is a method of remapping one IP address into another by examining the packet headers and modifying the address information within. This takes place in a router. Originally used for ease of rerouting traffic in IP networks without addressing every host, it has become a popular and essential tool in advanced NAT implementations featuring IP masquerading.

IP masquerading is a technique that hides an IP address space (e.g. your home network) behind a single (public) IP address. The outgoing address thus appears as though it has originated from the router, which must also do the reverse mapping when replies are received. The prevalence of IP masquerading is largely due to the limitations of the range of IPv4 addresses (as described at the beginning of this chapter) and the term NAT has become virtually synonymous with it.

Where is your data?

It may be on a local machine, on a local server or in "the cloud" (see Chapter 10 for a definition).

Cloud Computing is where the software and data do not reside on local servers, in the local organisation or possibly even in the same country. Whilst this frees up a lot of infrastructure and makes mobile computing more possible, it does have two main drawbacks:

The first is that a reliable network connection is essential to use the cloud.

The second is that the laws of data protection that apply to data are those that exist in the country in which the data resides: in the USA, for example, companies are allowed to sell the data they have on their network. Not to anyone, of course, but they can sell health records to insurance agencies, email addresses to marketers etc. So it is important, for health records, to know where the data is being held (see the GDPR, page 7). In the UK there is a G-Cloud, a cloud solution hosted here for public service use, thus making it subject to the UK's data protection laws. There are also more and more assured clouds being marketed.

In early 2018 NHS Digital published guidance on data off-shoring and cloud computing for health and social care. The main points are:

- *"NHS and Social care providers may use cloud computing services for NHS data. Data must only be hosted within the UK - European Economic Area (EEA), a country deemed adequate by the European Commission, or in the US where covered by Privacy Shield.*
- *Senior Information Risk Owners (SIROs) locally should be satisfied about appropriate security arrangements (using National cyber security essentials as a guide) in conjunction with Data Protection Officers and Caldicott Guardians.*
- *Help and advice from the Information Commissioner's Office is available and regularly updated.*
- *Changes to data protection legislation, including the General Data Protection Regulation (GDPR) from 25 May 2018, puts strict restrictions on the transfer of personal data, particularly when this transfer is outside the European Union. The ICO also regularly updates its GDPR Guidance."*[40]
- NHS Digital has provided some detailed guidance documents to support health and social care organisations.

Cloud computing is becoming more trusted. In January 2020 two NHS services moved to the cloud: The NHS e-Referral Service (e-RS) and the NHS 111 Directory of Services (DoS). The quoted benefits were the saving of public money while making the services more secure and efficient[41].

A good analysis of the issues can be found at http://www.save9.com/is-it-ok-to-backup-nhs-patient-data-in-the-cloud/. It's written from a supplier perspective so has a bias towards the advantages but is essentially correct – i.e. you can use cloud services, provided you do it in the right way (compliance with IG toolkit and the DP act plus local risk assessment for example).

Connecting medical devices to the hospital network

There are great advantages in connecting together ICT equipment to enable data sharing, together with the enhanced safety from a reduction in transcription errors and the increased availability and speed of access to information. However, this connectedness brings with it additional system security issues: a failure in one part may be swiftly replicated across the IT estate. There are many ways to tackle these issues and this section details some of these. It should be noted that best practice will utilise a range of security methods.

Firewalls

The first method is one of segregation, using a firewall. A firewall is, in the simplest sense, a pair of network cards (or a router) and a set of rules. A network packet arrives at one card, is tested against the rules and, if it passes, is passed to the other card for transmission. In this way, a part of a network can be protected from activity on the rest of the network by restricting the messages that can pass through it to a predefined and pre-approved set. The rules controlling this may be as simple as only allowing a predefined set of IP addresses through. Refinements include port numbers, the direction the message is travelling in, whether the incoming message is a response to an outgoing one (e.g. a web page) and specific exceptions to general rules. This is all achieved via packet filtering, where the header of the packet is examined in order to extract the information required for the rules.

The above description is of a hardware firewall. Software firewalls run on the device after the network traffic has been received. They can therefore be more sophisticated in their rules in that they can have access to additional information such as the program that made the request. Software firewalls can also include privacy controls and content filtering[xvi]. As the software firewall runs on the device, if the device becomes compromised then the firewall may also be compromised. The Windows 7 firewall only blocks incoming traffic, so for example it will not prevent a compromised device from sending malicious network packets. The Windows 10 firewall is similar: inbound connections to programs are blocked unless they are on the allowed list, outbound connections are allowed unless they match a rule. There are also Public and Private network profiles for the firewall controlling which programs can communicate on the private network as opposed to the Internet[xvii].

Bandwidth

Bandwidth in a computer network sense is its transmission capacity, which (as it is a function of the speed of transmission) is usually expressed in bps. The most common wired bandwidths are 1 Gbps (often called "Gigabit Ethernet"), 10 Mbps (standard Ethernet) and 100 Mbps (fast Ethernet). Wireless is generally slower – 802.11g supports up to 54 Mbps, for example[xviii]. As bandwidth is actually the capacity, binding together several cables can

---

[xvi] Although there are some very famous failures in this respect, such as filtering out images containing skin tone (not helpful in medicine) and the "Scunthorpe problem" where a part of a normal word triggers a filter rule.

[xvii] See https://www.online-tech-tips.com/windows-10/adjust-windows-10-firewall-settings/ for instructions on examining and adjusting the settings

[xviii] Note that these are maximums and a wired network stands a better chance of providing the full bandwidth due to less interference. 802.11g normally only provides 20Mbps and 802.11ac, operating in the 5GHz band, has a theoretical bandwidth of 1300Mbps but only provides 200Mbps. 802.11ax (also known as Wi-Fi 6) has a maximum of 14Gbps and also provides better throughput in high-density settings, such as corporate offices, airports and dense housing situations It requires the hardware to

increase the total bandwidth whilst not increasing the speed – although this would not normally be done in a departmental network, the point at which a hospital meets the national N3 network may be implemented this way (provided both sides of the connection can handle it – which is usually by routing pre-defined packets to specified lines, e.g. by IP address range).

It is never a good idea to reach 100% bandwidth utilisation and the average in order to avoid this may be as low as 30%, although 50% would be more common (see Figure 14). The amount of "spare" capacity is often termed "headroom". At 75% the throughput verses offered traffic curve starts to depart from a linear proportional increase of throughput for increase of offered traffic. At 80% the channel could be approaching overload. Much is dependent upon the traffic type - data traffic can cope with higher utilisation levels than voice as delay and jitter have more effect on the user experience for voice traffic than data traffic. Optimisation techniques such as QOS[xix] can be used to prioritise voice traffic (or any other traffic that is time-critical).

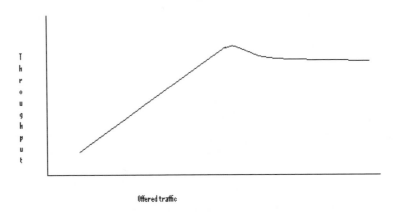

Figure 14: A Generalised Throughput verses Offered Traffic Curve Showing a Deterioration in Performance when Optimal Levels are Breached[42]

The above utilisation levels are generally for non collision based channels. In the case of Ethernet which uses CSMA[xx] with collision detection as the access mechanism, utilisation should be much lower. An overdriven CSMA channel can result in a throughput reduction rather than an increase with increasing offered traffic. Retrys as a result of a collision lead to more retrys and more collisions and so on. Collision detection with a limitation on the number of retrys and a back off between the retrys is intended to keep the channel stable but throughput will tail off. Kleinrock[43] provides good further reading.

The use of different network transport protocols can also improve throughput. For example, Skype uses TCP for video (which guarantees delivery) and UDP for audio (which doesn't). On first inspection this appears to be the wrong way round, but TCP waits until a missed packet is delivered, whereas UDP just carries on. Thus the video freezes whereas the audio doesn't – a small glitch in the audio feed (50fps) is not going to be noticed.

Wi Fi and Bluetooth suffer from interference, and the frequency range is the same as for microwave ovens. The reason that a frequency that excites water molecules and therefore is severely attenuated by them (e.g. people) was chosen was because it was available as no-one wanted it (for precisely those reasons).

---

be correctly set up in order to achieve anything better than 800Mbps though. This, however, does position wireless better as a method of provision.

[xix] **Quality-of-service**, a Cisco product.

[xx] **Carrier Sense Multiple Access**, a protocol in which a node verifies the absence of other traffic before transmitting on a shared transmission medium.

All the resilience methods outlined here require a level of redundancy: be it a copy, checksums or headroom. Thus a resilient system will always be over-engineered – in the case of bandwidth, over-engineering can remove the need for optimisation systems such as QOS, thus making the design (and therefore the support) simpler.

Infrastructure

The core of a modern hospital's infrastructure is the supervised, air-conditioned server room, with redundant power supply provision. The users link to this facility by Ethernet and offsite electronic replication is likely. The bulk of the front line data storage will use **Storage Area Network** (SAN) or **Network Attached Storage** (NAS) and the racks of servers will often be running virtual systems. Clinical Scientist/Engineer user specialists will have remote administrator access to their systems. Critical clinical systems, such as Radiotherapy facilities will be likely to have some form of segregation, such as VLAN[xxi]'s or firewalls. Virtual systems are particularly useful for enabling the local testing of commercial software upgrades, as it is relatively simple to destroy the server and re-create it.

Major components of a PC

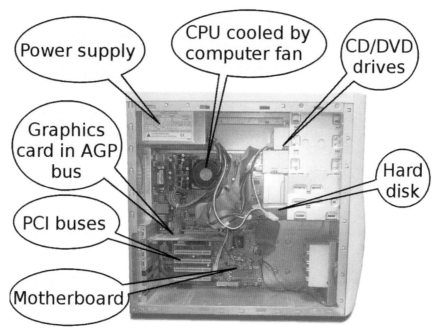

Figure 15: Inside a Standard PC[44]

Software

Software falls into one of three types:

1. Boot software – the stuff that gets the PC started.
2. **Operating system** (OS) – the stuff that does basic, but important things.
3. Applications – the stuff that does what you actually wanted a computer for in the first place.

The boot software is initiated when a computer starts up (either from power-on or a reset). It normally checks the hardware and then locates and loads an operating system (or, more likely, the loader for the OS). Dual (or larger) – boot systems will normally pause in order to ask the user which operating system they wish to use. The boot software is part of the hardware and is stored in **Read Only Memory** (ROM)[xxii]. Therefore one of the first things it

---

[xxi] Virtual LAN
[xxii] Originally bootstrap programs had to be keyed in by hand using switches on the front panel, in binary.

will do is to load drivers for the storage media that the OS is held on. It's the loader that asks you if you want to start Windows in safe mode, not the boot program.

Operating Systems
An operating system is a very complex piece of software that interfaces directly with the hardware upon which it is running. The first three introduced here are all multi-tasking operating systems which is why they are to be found on servers as well as end-user machines. The fourth has appeared more commonly in healthcare over the last decade, but mainly as an end-user system.

Microsoft Windows
There are two families of this operating system: end-user (such as Windows XP, Windows 10 and Windows 95) and server (normally dated, e.g. 2019, often with a release number, e.g. 2008 R2). Both may also be referred to by their service pack status, e.g. XP SP3 indicates Windows XP where service packs 1-3 have been applied.

Windows is a graphical user interface, employing the WIMP (**Windows, Icons, Mouse, Pointer** – although some variants interpret "M" as "menus" and "P" as "pull-down menus") paradigm pioneered by Xerox and brought into popularity by Apple and Atari. It is an event-driven operating system, in that events are generated (e.g. by a mouse click, a keyboard press, a timer or a USB device insertion) and these are offered by the operating system to the programs and processes that are currently running (including itself) for processing. For this reason a program may not necessarily cancel just because a user has clicked on a button labelled "Cancel" – the event will merely sit in a queue, awaiting processing.

Windows has gained great popularity, partly because of its relative openness for developers (compared to, say, Apple) but mostly due to its common user interface: similarly displayed buttons and icons perform similar functions across programs (e.g. the floppy disc icon for saving – even though the program is unlikely to be saving to a floppy disc) and almost-universal keyboard shortcuts (e.g. Ctrl-C for "copy"). This makes the learning of new programs easier and more intuitive.

Windows is most likely to be found running desktop end-user machines, departmental servers and (in its embedded form) medical devices.

Unix
Unix is also a family of operating systems and may also run on end-user machines as well as on servers. However, it is on the latter that it is now most prevalent, due to its robust stability. Whilst there are graphical user interfaces, it is most commonly accessed through a command-line interface, a "shell" (such as BASH, Bourne or C) that accepts certain commands (usually programs in their own right rather than embedded into the OS) and logic flow. Originally developed for dumb-terminal access (where all the user has is a keyboard and VDU and the processing takes place on the server) it can therefore be accessed easily via a terminal emulator on any end-user machine (e.g. a Windows PC or an Android phone).

A key concept in Unix is that of the pipe. In this, the output of one program can be "piped" as the input to the next in a chain, thereby producing complex processing from a set of relatively simple commands.

ls -al | more

A simple pipeline command, creating a long list of files which is then piped into the *more* command

ls -al | grep '^d'

As above, but lists only the directories, as *grep* (with these parameters) only shows the records that begin with the letter *d*

ls -al | grep Aug | grep -v '200[456]' | more

A complex example listing all Apache log files for the month of August excluding 2004-6[xxiii]

These examples[45] also introduce another key concept of Unix – that of regular expressions[xxiv], a simple example of which might be "randomi[sz]e" in a text search, which would match both spellings of the word (i.e. "randomise" and "randomize").

Unix is generally seen as an expensive operating system, which is one of the reasons it is less likely to be found on end-user machines. Unix is also most likely to be found running departmental and critical enterprise servers.

Linux

Linux was developed as an open-source variant of Unix by Linus Torvalds[46]. Its popularity rapidly increased because it is open-sourced and so developers are able to access the source code to the OS and produce new versions of the programs within it, thereby expanding functionality and correcting errors. The caveat is that this new version must also be freely available, with source code, to anyone who wishes to use it. There are therefore various different versions (referred to as "flavours") of Linux, such as Ubuntu and openSUSE.

As with Unix, Linux is mostly command-line, yet graphical user interfaces do exist and (as the cost factor does not exist) are more likely to be found on end-user machines. The low processing overhead (compared to Windows, for example) has led to the introduction of cheap yet powerful systems, such as the Raspberry Pi, which has seen Linux systems appearing in many areas of healthcare. Linux is most likely to be found running desktop end-user research machines, departmental servers and especially web servers.

iOS/macOS

iOS and macOS are OSs created and developed by Apple Inc. exclusively for its hardware. iOs is the mobile version (powering devices such as iPhone, iPad[xxv], and iPod) with macOS found on devices such as iMac and MacBook. They are very similar in terms of user experience, meaning that moving from one Apple device to another is very intuitive, once the first has been mastered (see the comment on Microsoft and standards, above).

Whereas macOS uses fairly traditional input devices such as a keyboard and a mouse, the iOS user interface is based upon direct manipulation, using multi-touch gestures such as swipe, tap, pinch, and reverse pinch which all have specific definitions within the context of the iOS OS and its multi-touch interface.

The tight development relationship between the hardware and software (compared to Linux which is designed to run on a vast range of hardware) means that both benefit from optimisations.

iOS is most likely to be found in mobile healthcare settings (such as clinical record taking) whereas macOS is more found in graphics-heavy settings, such as image processing. They are more likely to be end-user machines than servers, unless as part of an integrated system.

General

An operating system consists of a central part (often called the kernel) and a number of supplementary programs – this can especially be seen in UNIX-like OSs, where these supplementary programs can simply be replaced by a new executable and therefore the behaviour can be enhanced or corrected. An operating system is a very complex piece of software that interfaces directly with the hardware upon which it is running: all user software runs under the operating system and will call routines within the OS in order to achieve hardware effects, such as displaying information (on screen, printer or other display device), receiving input (from keyboard, mouse, graphics tablet, touch screen etc.) and reading from or writing to storage (hard discs, **Random Access Memory** (RAM) drives, tape systems or network-based storage).

---

xxiii Note that, contrary to what you might expect, the pattern in grep does not need to be inside quotation marks
xxiv Regular expressions pre-date Unix, but the syntax defined in Unix is now the most widely used.
xxv In 2019 iOS for iPad became iPadOS and at this point the OSs diverged.

Figure 16: The Operating System in a Hierarchy

It is possible to call OS routines directly from programs, for example to list all files with the extension .c in the current folder, using c:

```
struct _finddata_t c_file;
long hFile;

if ( (hFile = _findfirst("*.c", &c_file)) == -1L )
        printf("No *.c files in current directory");
else
{
        do
        {
                printf("%s\n", c_file.name);
        } while ( _findnext(hFile, &c_file) == 0 )
        _findclose(hFile);
}
```

Chapter 4 – Data

Data retention

Data retention times are one of the most confusing aspects of NHS data. There are multiple pages of guidance (110 pages in the guidance that was current until 29/7/16, this went to an Excel spreadsheet with 118 entries and is currently a pdf with 38 pages of guidance, plus many others of supporting information[47] (NHSX [online] (1))) and it can take several attempts to find the entry that best describes the data being retained. As records become more commonly electronic, there is a temptation to retain data indefinitely but this code gives instructions on disposal.

One important point of data retention is that when records identified for disposal are destroyed, a register of these records needs to be kept. (See the Records Management Code of Practice for Health and Social Care 2016 for further information[48])

An interesting question is what happens should data be kept beyond the recommended retention period. If it contains personal data then the GDPR's principle e (storage limitation) applies (see GDPR section) and the data must either be deleted or anonymised, otherwise there is the possibility of a fine. The exception to this is when it is being kept for public interest archiving, scientific or historical research, or statistical purposes.

If the data does not contain personal data then there appear to be no ramifications to keeping data beyond the retention limits.

Hospital Information Systems and Interfaces

The major hospital information system in use is the **Patient Administration System** (PAS), sometimes called an **Electronic Patient Record** (EPR)[i]. This system will handle all patient registrations, demographics, clinic appointments and admissions (planned and emergency). It will normally be the "gold standard" for data, in that it holds the "most correct" version, especially the demographics and GP contact information.

An EPR will have a heavy processing load. For this reason, it is common practice to have a second data repository which is a copy of the data, created via an overnight scheduled task. Reports may thereby be run against this data without incurring a performance hit on the main system. The data is at worst 24 hours out of date, but for most administrative reporting (as opposed to clinical reporting) this is acceptable. A notable exception is bed state reporting, which is therefore normally a feature of the main system.

The functionality of the EPR is greatly enhanced via interfaces to clinical systems. This will usually be via HL7 messages (see page 45) and may be outbound (where the data flow is from the EPR to the clinical system), inbound (the other direction) or two-way. Demographics are usually outbound, test results are usually inbound and bed state information may be two-way.

As the EPR will interface to many other systems, the use of an interface engine is usual. This may be thought of as a sophisticated router where outbound messages from all connected systems will be received and then passed to all relevant[ii] downstream systems for processing, usually for keeping databases synchronised. It can also process these messages, so that codes used by the EPR may be converted into ones used by the downstream system, for example.

An interface engine will normally include a large cache, so that downstream systems that go offline (e.g. for upgrade work) are able to collect the relevant messages when they come back on line. Therefore acknowledgement messages form an important part of the interface engine protocol.

The most recent move in the UK has been towards an **Electronic Health Record System** (EHRS) which contains all the information in an EPR but with additional data such as that from medical devices and specialised systems: it is a

---

[i] Technically there is a difference: A PAS consists of demographics and appointments, whereas an EPR contains the full medical record including correspondence. As PAS functionality increases, the distinction becomes blurred.

[ii] The relevance is normally determined via a set of rules.

longitudinal record bringing together patient data such as demographics and medical history, treatment information, diagnostic information, operational information[iii] and clinical care information. In doing so it provides a fuller picture of the patient pathway and provides opportunity for data mining such as operational and clinical analytics.

Equipment management database systems

An equipment management database system is, as the name implies, a database of equipment around which a system has been constructed to manage that equipment. As such, it shares a lot of features with asset management database systems but contains additional features to aid in the management of equipment, which for the focus of this book means medical equipment.

An asset management database will contain information such as the equipment name, manufacturer, purchase cost and date, replacement cost (and planned replacement date if known), location and a service history (if appropriate). Reports may then be run against this data to produce information on capital spend and assistance in forecasting future spend. It may also be used to highlight unreliable equipment, commonalities of purchasing (in order to assist in contract negotiations and bulk buying) and equipment loss due to theft or vandalism.

An equipment management database system will include all of these features, but will also include information so that the equipment may be managed appropriately. Probably the most common example of this additional functionality is the **Planned Preventative Maintenance** (PPM)[iv]. In order to implement PPMs, all equipment managed must be assigned a service plan. In its simplest form, this is a set time frame: for example, a set of scales that requires calibration once a year. A more complex plan might include different tests or calibrations to be performed at different times. This type of service plan will generally still include a fixed time interval, but will also include a service rotation. On the first rotation, it might be visually inspected to ensure that all seals are still in place. On the second rotation a calibration might be added and on the third a **Portable Appliance Test** (PAT) renewal might be undertaken in addition to inspection and calibration. The system will keep track of all work that is due (producing worklists for a particular time period), the service rotation that is due, parts and labour used in the maintenance and so on.

Inspecting, calibrating and testing all of a hospital's medical equipment is not a minor task: most such services spread the load across the entire year, which the management system is also able to assist in planning by reporting on peaks and troughs in the anticipated workload, adjusting for planned staff absences and potential peaks and troughs in emergency repairs (from historical data).

The system may also assist with functions such as the management of contracts (where equipment is maintained by a third party), the recording of repairs undertaken (thus determining when equipment has reached the end of its economic life) and the recording of medical device training.

In this latter example, all staff of the hospital are recorded along with the equipment they have been trained to use. Thus training can be kept current and a mechanism for preventing the unsafe use of equipment implemented.

In order to achieve all this functionality, an equipment management database system will need to be interfaced to other systems, such as a capital asset management system, a human resources system and a contracts management system.

Device tracking systems

Electronic tracking devices are a growing element of hospital practice and their role is considered here in terms of potential, rather than system design. The benefits of tracking devices are numerous, from the reduction in time

---

[iii] Appointments as opposed to surgery
[iv] Sometimes simply referred to as "servicing".

spent looking for equipment (estimated as being 2.5% of nurse time by UCLH in 2011[v]), to theft prevention. Other potential benefits are improved servicing due to having a reliable equipment asset register and the ability to run a more efficient equipment library.

Broadly, there are four types of technology to consider, as described in the table below. Each requires the asset to have a tag attached, which communicates with the central system. The tags may vary in size, depending on the amount of data required and the distance from the transponder that it is required to communicate with. This means that such a system may be deployed for multiple purposes. For example, it may describe bed occupancy, the stocking of a pharmacy cabinet or track the whereabouts of babies and/or vulnerable patients, as well as staff in lone working situations.

The required accuracy may also determine the technology: it is possible to "geofence" the organisation, so that tracked equipment is known to be within a "fenced area" but where it is within that area is unknown.

Technology	Description	Pros and cons
WiFi (Wireless Network)	This system uses an organisation's WiFi network (the same network that supports wireless computing devices). Tags transmit a WiFi signal, which is picked up by WiFi access points – if the signal is picked up by 4 or more access points, the location of the device can be triangulated in three dimensions. This may be supplemented by additional ultrasound "beacons" to more accurately locate devices within a particular room.	There is a claimed accuracy of location to 2m (although there exists some scepticism about this and it is probably only possible with the addition of ultrasound beacons). Makes use of an existing WiFi so no additional network is required. Fully scalable for patients, assets and staff. It requires many more WiFi access points than is needed just for wireless computing. Produces an additional load on the network. Tags are expensive (circa £65 each).

---

[v] Internal document, not externally published

Radio Frequency Identification (RFID)	A network of RFID receivers is positioned across the organisation, connected to the LAN. Tags (either active or passive) communicate with these receivers, which can track their location. Passive tags respond to a signal from gateways (from where they also draw their power to do so), whereas active ones will transmit data to a nearby receiver and have on-board power. This is a proven technology, being used in many industries, including retail, where cheap passive tags are attached to stock, and their location/presence is tracked	Tags are very cheap (passive tags are pennies each). The granularity of the mapping is not very precise. An additional network (of RFID transponders) is required.
RFID with **Infra-Red** (IR)	This uses RFID technology, supplemented by infra-red transmitters/detectors. IR can be used to track devices to a very granular level (bed space, or even a drawer), and information is then communicated centrally via an RFID network.	Accurate location of items at a very granular level. Fully scalable for patients, assets and staff. Additional network needs to be installed of RFID transponders. The solution is quite complex in that there are several technologies involved. The risk of failure is therefore higher.
Bluetooth	Bluetooth is a very short range communication protocol and so relies upon the tag being in the proximity of another device so enabled. It is very good for alerts (e.g. the tag has been separated from another device).	Whilst this technology has been around for a long time, it is the advent of the Apple AirTag, which links into Apple's Find My network that has made this viable in a hospital context. As it does not rely on fixed hardware such as RFID transponders, the granularity is dependent on the number of devices also on the Find My network.

			AirTags are small, contain their own power supply (a CR2032 battery) and cost about £100 for a pack of four – plus the cost of something to mount it in.

Figure 17: The four main technologies for asset tracking

Location tracking may, of course, be implemented as a side-effect of meeting another need: for example, connecting devices to a wi-fi network in order to remotely distribute drug libraries to infusion pumps. This requires triangulation to be added, but the infrastructure is already in place.

Radiology Information Systems (RIS) and PACS we will cover with DICOM (see page 54), which leaves us with HL7 and risk analysis & mitigation.

HL7

HL7 is a data exchange format. In order for computer systems to be able to process data produced by other systems, a data standard must be agreed. Even in proprietary systems from the same manufacturer the format of the data has to be consistent so that different modules can access that data and understand its meaning.

The simplest form of this is *positional meaning*. In this standard, the data will always consist of the same items in the same order (and each item may be of a fixed length). For example, the data below may be converted for transmission to an external system via the process shown in Figure 18 to Figure 20.

Surname	Forename	Address	e-mail
Snail	Brian	Magic Roundabout	brian@roundabout.com
Flowerpot	Bill	Garden	bill@weed.co.uk
Cat	Bagpuss	Shop Window	bagpuss@catworld.net
Miller	Windy	The Windmill, Trumpton	wmiller@chigley.ac.uk

Figure 18: A Set of Data, Arranged in a Table

The items in the first row are field names (but may also be thought of as column headings).

Surname	9
Forename	7
Address	22
Email	22

Figure 19: The Maximum Length of the Data in Each Field

Snail^^^^Brian^^Magic Roundabout^^^^^^brian@roundabout.com^^FlowerpotBill^^^Garden^^^^^^^^^^^^^^^^bill@weed.co.uk^^^^^^^^^Cat^^^^^^BagpussShop Window^^^^^^^^^^^bagpuss@catworld.net^^Miller^^^Windy^^The Windmill, Trumptonwmiller@chigley.ac.uk

Figure 20: The Data Converted into One Long Data Stream

Note that unused characters are rendered with ^ and not as spaces, as these appear in the data itself.

Whilst the advantages of this system for data sharing are obvious[vi], so are the limitations[vii].

In order to overcome these, we might introduce a header to the data stream that describes the data that is to follow. Such a header might, for this example, be:

4^Surname^9^Forename^7^Address^22^e-mail^22^

This header first states the number of items per record (and thus also the number of items in the header), then the name and length of each field in turn, all separated by a special character. Extensions to this to describe the type of data (numeric, currency, textual, boolean etc.) are also possible[viii]. It is important to know the data type as 3/4 may be a fraction, a date, a time signature or just text. Phone numbers require the leading zero as they are not really numbers but text (to answer that question, Matt Parker suggests[49] asking what half of the value means – if it's meaningless, it's probably not a number) and MARCH5 may be a date or a gene. Simply importing this data into Excel (which physicists would never do…) strips the meaning and replaces them with erroneous data.

DICOM is a tagged file format. A tagged version of the example above is shown below. It can be seen from this example that a tagged format is not particularly suitable for data sets which are comprised of multiple rows, as the tags appear in each row and therefore are repeated throughout the data stream. However, it is very flexible and efficient for single data item files (e.g. an image or a music file) as only the tags that have values are required to be present and additional tags can easily be incorporated.

4^Surname^9^Forename^7^Address^22^e-mail^22^Snail^^^^Brian^^Magic
Roundabout^^^^^^brian@roundabout.com^^FlowerpotBill^^^Garden^^^^^^^^^^^^^^^bill@weed.co.uk^^^^^
^^^^

Figure 21: The first two records of the data stream from before, complete with header.

Surname^9^Snail^^^^Forename^7^Brian^^Address^22^Magic Roundabout^^^^^^e-mail^22^
brian@roundabout.com^^ Surname^9^Flowerpot Forename^7^Bill^^^ Address^22^Garden^^^^^^^^^^^^^^^
e-mail^22^ bill@weed.co.uk^^^^^^^^^EOF

Figure 22: the same data stream, in a tagged format[ix].

Interfaces
An interface is a point where two systems, subjects, organisations, etc. meet and interact. In computing, an interface is a shared boundary across which two or more separate components of a computer system exchange information. The exchange can be between software, computer hardware, peripheral devices, humans or combinations of these.

We can therefore see that there are several types of interface which we might be interested in:
- User interface, where the user interacts with the software.
- Hardware interface, where electronic components interact.
- Software interface, where software components[x] interact.
- Systems interface, where software systems interact in order to pass information (synchronisation and interrogation).

For the purpose of this chapter we will turn our attention to the last example.

[vi] Simplicity is the main one – the simpler the system the more likely it is to be implemented
[vii] For example, consider adding just one field to the table, or increasing the length of a field
[viii] The dBase 3 file format is a good place to start.
[ix] Note the "EOF" indicating the end of the stream. Also that the order of the fields is now unimportant as they are prefixed by their tag in all cases.
[x] Bear in mind that an operating system is software

We now need to consider the exchange of incremental changes within a database. This case is very common in healthcare where many clinical systems take a "feed" from the PAS and return results to it. Here the PAS exchanges small changes such as date of appointment, time of arrival at reception etc., as well as large ones such as a new patient being registered (although, in a database of over a million patients this may also be considered "small").

Such incremental changes are achieved through a messaging interface and the most common standard adopted for these is HL7. Note that this is not "Health Language Seven" as some translate it – the "Level 7" refers to the position it occupies in the OSI 7-layer model – the application layer.

The OSI 7-layer model

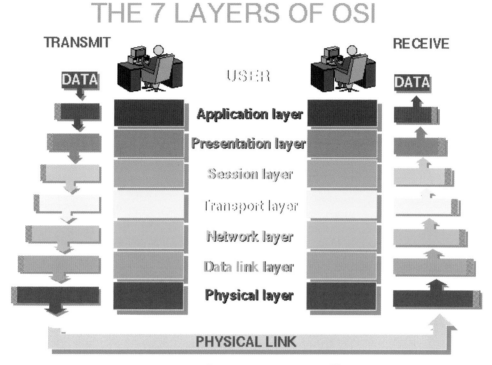

Figure 23: The Seven Layer OSI Model[50]

The OSI 7-layer model describes the transmission of messages. In sending a message, each layer (from the highest – the Application – to the lowest – the Physical) adds a wrapper to the message, which is removed after physical transmission as the message makes its way back up the layers into the receiving application.

The **physical layer (1)**, the lowest layer of the OSI model, is concerned with the transmission and reception of the unstructured raw bit stream over a physical medium. It describes the electrical/optical, mechanical, and functional interfaces to the physical medium, and carries the signals for all of the higher layers. It deal with such matters as which signal state represents a binary 1, how many pins are on a connector (and what they do) and how many volts/db should be used to represent a given signal state.

The **data link layer (2)** provides error-free transfer of data frames from one node to another over the physical layer, allowing layers above it to assume virtually error-free transmission over the link. This layer is the protocol layer, providing the functional and procedural means to transfer data between network entities. The data link layer handles matters such as establishing and terminating the logical link between two nodes, transmitting/receiving frames sequentially and determining when the node "has the right" to use the physical medium (see the description of "token ring" on page 29).

The **network layer (3)** controls the operation of the subnet, deciding which physical path the data should take based on network conditions, priority of service, and other factors. It is concerned with routing, subnet traffic control and logical-physical address mapping.

The **transport layer (4)** ensures that messages are delivered error-free, in sequence, and with no losses or duplications[xi]. It relieves the higher layer protocols from any concern with the transfer of data between them and their peers. It handles such matters as message segmentation, message acknowledgement and session multiplexing[xii]. (A *session* is "*a semi-permanent interactive information interchange, also known as a dialogue, a conversation or a meeting, between two or more communicating devices, or between a computer and user.*"[51]).

The **session layer (5)** allows session establishment between processes running on different stations. It handles session establishment, maintenance and termination, allowing two application processes on different machines to establish, use and terminate a session[xiii].

The **presentation layer (6)** formats the data to be presented to the application layer. It can be viewed as the translator for the network. This layer may translate data from a format used by the application layer into a common format at the sending station, then translate the common format to a format known to the application layer at the receiving station. It handles code conversions such as ASCII to EBCDIC[xiv], bit-order and **Carriage Return/Line Feed** pairs (CR/LF). Data compression and encryption take place at this layer.

The **application layer (7)** serves as the window for users and application processes to access network services. This layer contains a variety of commonly needed functions such as resource sharing, remote printing and file access and directory services.

Further HL7

HL7 is administered by Health Level Seven International[52], a not-for-profit **American National Standards Institute** (ANSI)-accredited organisation. Although HL7 develops conceptual standards, document standards and application standards, it is only the messaging standard that we will consider here.

Version 2 of HL7 was established in 1987 and went through various revisions (up to 2.7). Version 2 is backwards-compatible, in that a message that adheres to 2.3 is readable in a 2.6-compliant system.

Version 3 (the latest version) appeared in 2005 and, unlike v2, is based on a formal methodology (the **HL7 Development Framework**, or HDF) and object-oriented principles. The HDF "*documents the processes, tools, actors, rules, and artifacts relevant to development of all HL7 standard specifications, not just messaging.*[53]" As such it is largely **Universal Modelling Language** (UML) compliant, although there are currently exceptions.

The cornerstone of the HL7 v3 development process is the **Reference Information Model** (RIM). It is an object model created as part of the Version 3 methodology, consisting of a large pictorial representation of the clinical data. It explicitly represents the connections that exist between the information carried in the fields of HL7 messages. An HL7 v3 message is based on an XML encoding syntax. As such it is far more versatile than v2, but with an attendant overhead. Due to the installed userbase of v2 and the difference in message structure, v3 is not yet in

---

[xi] Similar in description to the data link layer, but handling the logical data rather than physical.

[xii] Placing several message streams, or sessions onto one logical link and keeping track of which messages belong to which sessions

[xiii] It is probably simplest to envisage a session as being a connection.

[xiv] ASCII and EBCDIC are two numerical methods of representing characters, e.g. "A" is ASCII 65 and EBCDIC 193. ASCII actually consists of four 32-character alphabets. The first (numbered zero, of course) is control characters such as horizontal tab and end of transmit block. Next is punctuation marks, then upper case letters and finally lower case letters. There are 32 due to 7-bit binary. The "spare" slots are used for additional punctuation marks with the last character (127) being delete – on paper tape that was 7 punched holes which was a deletion you can't just hit "undo" on.

widespread use. A very good comparison of the two formats can be found at http://www.ringholm.de/docs/04300_en.htm, of which a small part is reproduced in Figure 24 and Figure 25.

```
PID|||555-44-4444||EVERYWOMAN^EVE^E^^^^L|JONES|19620320|F|||153 FERNWOOD DR.^
^STATESVILLE^OH^35292||(206)3345232|(206)752-121||||AC555444444||67-A4335^OH^20030520<cr>
```

Figure 24: A Section of a HL7 v2.4 Message, Detailing the Patient a Test is For

```
<recordTarget>
  <patientClinical>
  <id root="2.16.840.1.113883.19.1122.5" extension="444-22-2222"
     assigningAuthorityName="GHH Lab Patient IDs"/>
  <statusCode code="active"/>
   <patientPerson>
    <name use="L">
      <given>Eve</given>
      <given>E</given>
      <family>Everywoman</family>
    </name>
    <asOtherIDs>
      <id extension="AC555444444" assigningAuthorityName="SSN"
         root="2.16.840.1.113883.4.1"/>
    </asOtherIDs>
   </patientPerson>
  </patientClinical>
 </recordTarget>
```

Figure 25: A Similar Section to the Message in Figure 24, Using HL7 v3

A further layer of data exchange is **Cross-enterprise Document Sharing** (XDS) which allows structured data documents of any type to be shared across platforms. Key elements in this are the document source (e.g. an EPR), the document repository (a shared store) and the document registry (essentially an index on the documents). Because the data is structured, the registry is able to index not only the title or metadata from within a header, but the data contained within the document itself. This makes searching the registry more powerful. XDS is of particular interest in a healthcare setting where the source material may be produced from a large range of systems and devices (e.g. for a PACS or an EPR).

Fast Healthcare Interoperability Resources (FHIR)
FHIR is the global industry standard for passing healthcare data between systems. It is free, open, and designed to be quick to learn and implement. FHIR is part of an international family of standards developed by HL7, combining the best features of HL7's v2, v3 and CDA[xv] products[xvi] together with the latest web standards (XML, JSON, HTTP, OAuth, etc). There is a strong focus on implementability. The information models and APIs developed using this standard provide a means of sharing health and care information between providers and their systems regardless of the setting that care is delivered in.

[xv] Clinical Document Architecture
[xvi] Thus providing an evolutionary development path from HL7 Version 2 and CDA: these standards can co-exist and use each other

NHS Digital is making extensive use of the HL7 FHIR standard, doing so across the different areas that FHIR supports, which include:

- FHIR ReSTful APIs
- FHIR Documents
- FHIR Messages

Products developed by NHS Digital make use of a consistent set of FHIR profiles and specifications, a number of which are already published. Current specifications include Transfer of Care and CareConnect.

The HL7 UK FHIR Reference Server is available at https://fhir.hl7.org.uk/ and includes FHIR profiles designed to be used across the country.

Profiles used within NHS digital created solutions are published on the Reference Server at https://fhir.nhs.uk/.

Figure 26: The FHIR Structure[xvii]

This simple example shows the important parts of a resource: a local extension (orange), the human readable HTML presentation (magenta), and the standard defined data content (blue).

Further information on the FHIR is at http://www.hl7.org/fhir/index.html

---

[xvii] From http://www.hl7.org/fhir/summary.html

Risk Analysis & Mitigation

Possibly the largest change to IEC601 in the publication of the third edition is the requirement for manufacturers to have a formal risk management system that conforms to ISO 14971:2007[xviii] in place.

A risk management system includes within it two key concepts:

- Acceptable levels of risk
- Residual risk

Once acceptable levels of risk have been established, all residual risks (as documented in the hazard log – a part of the risk management file) can be measured against them. That way, risks can be demonstrably determined to be acceptable prior to manufacture and certainly prior to deployment. These also link nicely into the DCBs 0129 and 0160 described on page 24.

Risk management responses can be a mixture of four main actions:

- Transfer – where the current score is higher than an acceptable target score the decision reached may be to transfer the consequence of a risk to another owner, e.g. purchase an insurance policy so that financial loss is covered.
- Tolerate – where the current score is within an acceptable limit the decision reached may be to tolerate or accept the risk with no further action required. In this case the controls must be monitored and the risk reviewed regularly.
- Treat – where the current score is higher than an acceptable score the decision reached may be to treat the risk. A SMART action plan will be developed, and when an action is complete the current score should be reviewed. The risk should be reviewed regularly.
- Terminate – where the current score is higher than an acceptable score and there is no option to transfer, tolerate or treat the risk, the decision reached may be to NOT proceed with the activity. In this case the only option is to choose to terminate the risk.

Safety Cases

The purpose of a safety case

A clinical safety case report is a version controlled document, produced to support a specific product/system/activity/project phase/gate. The report presents a summary of the key components of the safety case relating to the safety of the product up to this point of its lifecycle with references to supporting information. It forms part of the risk management records, and may be made available to an assessor or regulatory authority. It can be produced at any point in the software lifecycle prior to release, although "design" or "development" are the best options for initial construction, with "testing" providing the evidence for the case.

The safety case report is a structured argument, supported by a body of evidence, intended to provide a compelling, comprehensible and valid case that a system or part of a system is acceptably safe in the given context.

This report is a means of communication with all stakeholders including suppliers, customers, end users, top management and regulators, as appropriate. The content is a summary of relevant knowledge which has been acquired during development or use and which relates to the safety of the product and its use. The report identifies the methods and techniques employed to derive that knowledge and the criteria employed to justify the acceptance of the residual risks.

Prior to safety cases being introduced to the healthcare sector, the method of determining if a system was safe was through the measurement of harm via falls data, never events etc. This relied on outcome measures with little understanding of how the outcome came about, as well as being reactive rather than proactive due to the use of

---

[xviii] Medical devices – Application of risk management to medical devices

historical data only. A safety case, however, is a proactive technique as the risks are identified and assessed prior to the system being implemented. It is a risk-based argument containing the supporting evidence of the system operating at a specified safety level[54].

It is not unusual for a safety case to be constructed while the project is still in progress. In fact, the safety case report can be an important piece of evidence in getting approval to "go live".

A hazard workshop therefore needs to identify hazards that may appear (e.g. "lack of time to complete login module causes security breach") and mitigations that have not yet been applied (this is especially true of acceptance testing) as well as ones already in place.

A safety case report is a living document that gets updated as the project progresses, therefore it can point to testing that is planned to be done, and, once done, update the safety case appropriately (e.g. "testing demonstrated no errors in dose calculation, but did reveal a potential security flaw in the login procedure").

At the heart of risk analysis and safety cases lies the hazard log, so we will examine this now.

Hazard Log

A hazard log is a record keeping tool applied to tracking all hazard analysis, risk assessment and risk reduction activities for the whole-of-life of a safety-related system. Important aspects of its disposition and use are:

- It is the single source of record for all risk management activities. Where necessary it cross-references other documents to demonstrate how hazards have been resolved
- It is the primary mechanism for providing objective evidence of the risk management process and assurance of the effective management of hazards and accidents
- It is continuously updated throughout the project lifecycle (including decommissioning and disposal)
- It is first created as an outcome of the preliminary hazard analysis process
- It is typically maintained by a systems assurance manager throughout a project's development and assessment phases
- It is formally closed at the completion of a contracted development and handed over to the system owner
- It is preserved into a system's operation and maintenance phases to support functional safety management of maintenance and enhancement activities.

Chambers.com.au notes: "*A hazard log is deemed to be closed out when the safety risks associated with all hazards identified have been reduced to a level that is acceptable to the system owner.*" (NB reduced, not eliminated) It also offers this as a sample hazard:

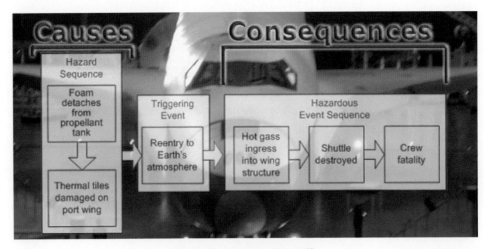

Figure 27: A sample hazard[55]

A hazard log is simply a record, normally in tabular form, containing the following:

Hazard Record Structure[xix]

Field	Description
Hazard number	A unique identifier so that this hazard can be referred to in the safety case report
Issue/risk description	A short description of the risk or issue. This may reference a longer description
Cause	The cause of the risk, e.g. poor manufacture, faulty design
Consequences	The consequence of the risk or issue manifesting itself
Risk Rating	A risk score composed of three parts: the Severity (1-5 where 5 is the worst) the Likelihood (1-5 where 5 is the most likely) the Score (the product of the other two numbers)
Mitigations	A description of actions that either reduce the severity (e.g. battery power instead of mains) or likelihood (e.g. staff training)
Post-mitigation Risk Rating	A risk score composed of three parts: the Severity (1-5 where 5 is the worst) the Likelihood (1-5 where 5 is the most likely) the Score (the product of the other two numbers)
Evidence	A description of the evidence that the mitigation has been successfully applied
GSN reference	A unique reference number to an element in the GSN diagram (i.e. it is unique to the GSN – it may occur repeatedly in this table)

Figure 28: Hazard record structure

There are many ways of enumerating risk in order to produce the risk rating. There is an illustrative example in NHS Digital's implementation guidance that accompanies the DCB0129 and DCB 0160 standards[56] and for software, a very good one is outlined in Scope 28:2[57] which includes enumeration methods such as "the greater the number of users the greater the chance of the software being used in an inappropriate way".

A hazard log is normally produced during a hazard workshop. This workshop is normally chaired by a suitably qualified and experienced safety expert who has also been tasked with writing (or signing off) the safety case.

A hazard workshop should contain people closely associated with the issue or system being discussed. For a clinical software system, this will include users of the system as well as people from the clinical environment in which it is to be used (who may, of course, be the same group).

[xix] This hazard record format is fairly typical, for example it is the same structure as used by the UK Civil Aviation Authority (CAA), which can itself be downloaded from the internet as a template document (CAA, 2013); https://www.caa.co.uk/WorkArea/DownloadAsset.aspx?id=4294971016

The main questions to address are:

- What might go wrong? (NB "might" not "has" – the workshop should think widely)
- How likely is this to happen?
- What are the effects if it does?
- What can be done to reduce the likelihood and/or effect?
- What is the likelihood after this mitigation?
- What are the effects after this mitigation?

From these answers the hazard log and then safety case can be constructed.

Chapter 5 – The DICOM Model

This chapter introduces the DICOM model for representing real-world attributes of medical imaging data. You can find the DICOM Standard online[58]. It's a long document of over 5,000 pages. The aim of this chapter is to explain some concepts to help to navigate it. You might like to download a copy of parts 3 and 6 of the standard to browse as you read this.

Images in context

An image contains a set of measurements made at multiple spatial locations.

Images show the spatial relationship between values. Measurements are made at different locations, and their relative positions are preserved and mapped into an image. The locations are often (though not always) arranged on a rectangular grid. We sometimes use the term pixel - or its three-dimensional counterpart voxel - to describe the volume of space around each location.

The measurement itself depends on the modality. For example, an x-ray image is formed by measuring attenuation, while an MRI image measures proton density (usually weighted with other factors too). Some measurements are scalar, such as CT density; others have multiple values per pixel, such as a colour photograph or MRI **Diffusion Tensor Imaging** (DTI). Measurements may come from small spatial volumes, like voxels in a CT image (tomographic imaging), or they may be aggregated along a line, like pixels in a plain film x-ray (projection imaging).

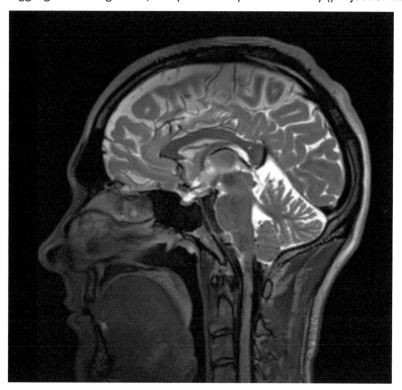

Figure 29: An MRI Image

To make meaningful clinical use of a medical image, like the one above, you need to know a number of extra things about it. First what kind measurement it contains - where it fits on the various axes above. Next you need some facts about the patient: their name, identifying numbers, perhaps their date of birth and diagnosis. You'll also need to know where and when the image was acquired, by whom and with what equipment. You need a record of the parameters used: if this was an MRI scan, what was the echo time? The flip angle? It's essential to understand the image's orientation and spatial scaling, which body part was imaged (is this the left or right arm?), and the patient's position while the image was taken. You may want to know where and when it was archived, who requested the scan, whether a radiological report has been authorised and - if so - what it concluded. And so on and so on.

These pieces of 'extra information' are called metadata. Metadata are the supporting details allowing meaningful clinical use of an image.

The DICOM standard describes how to store both the image itself (an array of pixels or voxels) and a wide variety of these real-world metadata.

Modelling images with DICOM

DICOM is a large and complex standard, thousands of pages describing thousands of distinct metadata elements. Scientists often first encounter DICOM as a file format, but it is helpful to consider the standard as presenting two distinct things:

1. An information model for clearly describing all the real-world concepts in medical imaging.
2. A technical implementation to turn this model into bytes for storage or network exchange.

DICOM is designed to operate safely across big, distributed, multi-vendor networks of imaging devices. For this to work, both the information model and the technical implementation have to be clearly defined. This chapter focusses on the information model.

Creating structure with Information Entities

The key to understanding this complexity is recognising that DICOM has a strongly structured, hierarchical model for representing imaging metadata.

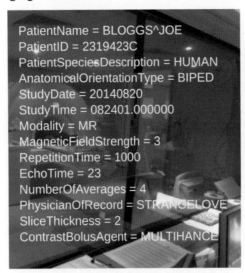
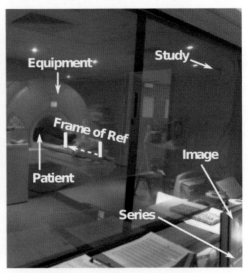

An unstructured model   A structured model

Figure 30: Unstructured verses Structured Models

If you've ever worked with DICOM files, you may have dumped their content and seen a list something like the left-hand view above. This might give the impression that DICOM attaches a long list of arbitrary facts to each image, some important, others very specialised; a mixture of facts relating to the patient, scanner, imaging configuration, and hospital imaging referral.

Actually, though, this apparently flat list of facts is organised into a hierarchical structure. DICOM views the world as a collection of **Information Entities** (IEs), each representing a distinct real-world concept: we'll consider six of the most important ones in this chapter, shown in the right-hand view above.

The hierarchy of IEs looks like this:

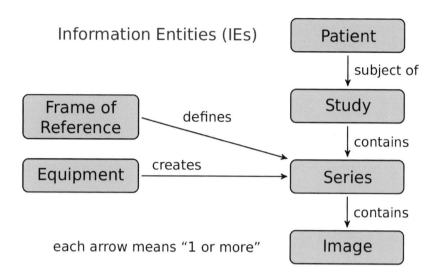

Figure 31: Information Entities

In this model, the column down the right-hand side is the hierarchy usually shown by the study browser on a scanner or PACS:

- A *Patient* represents a person being imaged
- A *Study* represents a set of related images and data, often associated with a single scanning visit
- A *Series* represents a stack of images acquired together, with many properties in common, such as the slices of a 3D CT volume or a single T1-weighted multislice MRI acquisition
- An *Image* contains an array of pixels - more generally this is called an *Instance*, as it may be a non-image object such as a structured report or annotation

Each series then has two other associated IEs:

- An item of *Equipment* is a scanner (or other system) creating the series
- A *Frame of Reference* represents a patient positioned in a single co-ordinate system: when several series share a frame of reference, pixels with matching co-ordinates will be at same spatial position within the patient

Collecting entities with Information Object Definitions

IEs are abstract concepts. For each specific use case, such as MRI or CT images, DICOM has an **Information Object Definition** (IOD).

An IOD defines the exact set of DICOM Attributes (individual facts) to be present in this class of IE. For an MR Image, the Image IE contains some MR-specific parameters like echo time, flip angle and so on. These wouldn't be relevant for a CT Image: instead you would find **Peak kiloVoltage** (KVP), revolution time, etc.

Most devices handling an MR Image will also need details of the patient, study, equipment and so on. The DICOM standard allows for this by including content from both the specific IE of interest (the Image) and the other IEs which provide context. An IOD which defines a collection of attributes across the whole hierarchy of IEs is called a Composite IOD: this is the type we'll encounter most often in working with imaging data[i].

---

[i] The standard also uses normalised IODs to define the attributes of certain individual IEs without context. These are rarely encountered in day-to-day work with imaging data.

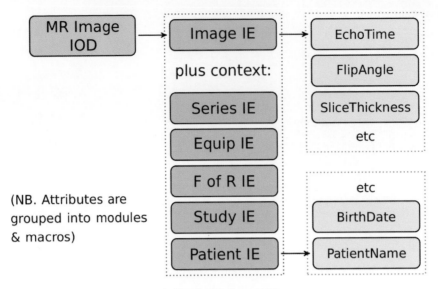

Figure 32: MR Image IOD

This is illustrated by the *MR Image IOD* pictured above. The composite IOD contains the image IE plus all five other IEs which give it context. Each of these is further broken down into a list of attributes: some generic (such as slice thickness in the image IE, or date of birth in the patient IE) and others specific to the MR use case (such as flip angle).

To avoid repetition, the DICOM standard collects related attributes typically used together into *modules*. Both IODs and modules are defined in Part 3 of the standard[ii]:

- **Part 3 Annex A** defines composite IODs, showing which modules should be included in each IE
- **Part 3 Annex C** defines modules, showing which attributes they contain, and explaining their use and meaning

[ii] The entire DICOM standard is known as NEMA standard PS3, so you will sometimes see part 3 referenced to as PS3.3, part 4 as PS3.4 and so on.

Let's follow the current example through the standard. Part 3 section A.4.3 defines the MR *image IOD* like this:

IE	Module	Reference	Usage
Patient	Patient	C.7.1.1	M
	Clinical Trial Subject	C.7.1.3	U
Study	General Study	C.7.2.1	M
	Patient Study	C.7.2.2	U
	Clinical Trial Subject	C.7.2.3	U
Series	General Series	C.7.3.1	M
	Clinical Trial Series	C.7.3.2	U
Frame of Reference	Frame of Reference	C.7.4.1	M
Equipment	General Equipment	C.7.5.1	M
Image	General Image	C.7.6.1	M
	Image Plane	C.7.6.2	M
	Image Pixel	C.7.6.3	M
	Contrast/Bolus	C.7.6.4	C *
	Device	C.7.6.12	U
	Specimen	C.7.3.22	U
	MR Image	C.8.3.1	M
	Overlay Plane	C.9.2	U
	VOI LUT	C.11.2	U
	SOP Common	C.12.1	M
	Common Instance Reference	C.12.2	U

* mandatory if contrast media was used in this image

Figure 33: MR Image IOD[iii]

Each of the IEs down the left-hand side includes a series of modules, either Mandatory (M), User-defined (U) which means optional, or Conditional (C) in which case the conditions are specified.

Each module then defines an actual list of attributes to be included. Let's look at the *MR image* module, found in part 3 section C.8.3.1 and a mandatory part of the IOD above. Here are a few rows extracted from this module definition:

[iii] All tables in this chapter are adapted from those in the DICOM standard

Attribute Name	Tag	Type	Description
Image Type	(0008,0008)	1	Image identification characteristics, see C.8.3.1.1.1 for detail.
Scanning Sequence	(0018,0020)	1	Type of data taken: **SE:** Spin Echo **IR:** Inversion Recovery **GR:** Gradient Recalled **EP:** Echo Planar **RM:** Research Mode
MR Acquisition Type	(0018,0023)	2	Data encoding scheme: **2D:** freq x phase **3D:** freq x freq x phase
Repetition Time	(0018,0080)	2C	Period between the beginning of a pulse sequence and the next (essentially identical) sequence. Required when Scanning Sequence is EP and Sequence Variant is not SK.
Imaging Frequency	(0018,0085)	3	Precession frequency in MHz of the nucleus being addressed.

Figure 34: Part of the MR Image Module Definition

So now we can follow through the standard to construct a complete list of attributes required in the MR image IOD - and as you'll see above, the standard contains further explanatory text for any attributes needing it.

We will explore the Tag and Type properties in the next section.

Attributes
The basic building block of the DICOM information model is the *attribute*.

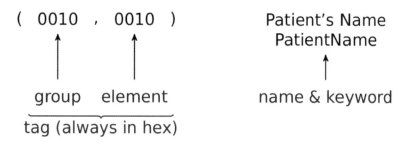

Figure 35: Structure of an Attribute

Each attribute has several properties:

- A **Name**, as shown in the table above. DICOM implementations should use the standardised name wherever possible for consistency.
- A **Keyword**, a version of the name simplified to have no spaces, punctuation, or confusing possessives (for example the attribute called *Patient's Name* has keyword form *PatientName*). This is intended for programmatic implementations, such as DICOM-handling libraries.
- A **Tag**, which is a numeric identifier for the attributes: it consists of two four-digit hexadecimal[iv] numbers: the group and element numbers.
- A **Type**, indicating whether the value is mandatory or optional:
  - Type 1 attributes must be present, with a valid value
  - Type 2 attributes must be present, but if no meaningful value exists they may be zero-length for "no value"
  - Type 3 attributes are optional
  - Type 1C or 2C attributes are conditional, with the conditions specified in the standard. (They are not optional: if the conditions are met, they are treated as type 1 or 2 attributes and must be present; if the conditions are not met, they must not be present.)
- A **Value Representation** (VR), indicating the type of data held in the attribute; for example, a string, integer or date. (This is analogous to data type in programming.)
- A **Value Multiplicity** (VM), indicating how many values this attribute contains: values can be scalar or vector. The VM may be a single number, a range, or an unbounded range like *1-n*. (This is analogous to *array length* in programming.)

Every standard attribute's Name, Keyword, Tag, VR and VM are listed in the *DICOM Data Dictionary* found in Part 6 of the standard.

An attribute's type can vary between IODs: the same attribute could be mandatory (type 1) for an MR image but optional (type 3) for another type of image. So the type isn't specified in the dictionary, instead it's a column in the module definition as shown in the *MR image* example above from part 3 section C.8.3.1 of the standard.

[iv] Hexadecimal is a counting system with 16 digits, 0-9 and A-F; so your DICOM element numbers can look like like 0010 and 07FE.

Value Representations

DICOM defines a large list of possible VRs. Each is indicated by a two-letter uppercase code - there's a complete list in part 5 section 6.2. Here are a few common examples:

VR	Name	Contained type
DT	Date Time	String of form YYYYMMDDHHMMSS.FFFFFF
DS	Decimal String	Float as up to 16-character string
LO	Long String	Up to 64-character string
US	Unsigned Short	16-bit unsigned binary integer
FL	Floating Point Single	32-bit IEEE floating point number
UI	Unique Identifier (UID)	Up to 64-character UID comprising numbers 0-9 and .
PN	Person Name	SURNAME^FIRST^MIDDLE^PREFIX^SUFFIX; separator may be omitted for empty trailing components
SQ	Sequence	Sub-list of DICOM attribute sets

Figure 36: Example Value Representations

There are many more VRs, and the standard defines the exact semantics, character set, and allowed length of each.

Sequence Attributes

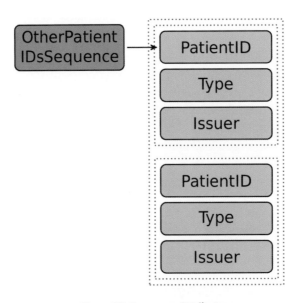

Figure 37: Sequence Attributes

DICOM attributes can be nested: when an attribute's VR is SQ it contains other attributes.

Each attribute (uniquely identified by its tag) can only appear once in a DICOM dataset. Sequence attributes allow us to circumvent this rule: each SQ attribute contains multiple child datasets, and each child dataset contains multiple attributes.

In the example above, a sequence attribute is used to represent additional hospital IDs for a patient, perhaps issued by other institutions. Each additional ID has several attributes, including the ID itself and the ID's issuer: the sequence allows us to encode an arbitrary number of these little datasets, one for each additional ID.

Private Attributes

In an attribute's tag, the *group* number indicates who is responsible for defining the attribute's use:

- If the group is even, the attribute must be listed in the DICOM standard
- If the group is *odd* [v], the attribute is *private*, declared and used by a particular vendor

Vendors are not obliged to document the purpose of their private attributes (although of course it is helpful when they do so!). The technical encoding of attributes allows DICOM readers to skip over private attributes whose meaning is unknown to them, while still reading all standard attributes in a dataset.

Because there is no central registry of private tags, it would be possible for two vendors to use the same tag for different purposes. To avoid these conflicts, the DICOM standard has a mechanism for reserving blocks for private attributes using a *Private Creator Tag*.

Private creator tags are put in the bottom section of the group: for group gggg they must be between (gggg,0010) and (gggg,00FF). The last two digits of the chosen element then define the other elements reserved: if the private creator is written to (gggg,0014), then all tags (gggg,1400) to (gggg,14FF) in this particular DICOM dataset are reserved for this vendor.

This table shows a concrete example of a real private block:

(0051,0012)	"SIEMENS MR HEADER"
(0051,120A)	"TA 06:05"
(0051,1212)	"TP 0"

Figure 38: An example of a private block

Although the meaning of these private attributes isn't published, some simple experimentation shows that TA is the acquisition time and TP the table position. Table position isn't always at tag (0051,1212): rather it's always at (0051,xx12) with xx set by the last two digits of the private creator tag containing the string "SIEMENS MR HEADER". You may sometimes see this "xx" notation in descriptions of element numbers to show that a private attribute conforms with this use.

Older versions of the standard lacked the private creator reservation mechanism, so you may still sometimes encounter odd-numbered groups without identified creators.

The lowest-numbered odd groups 0001, 0003, 0005 and 0007 may not be used for private tags.

---

[v] A hexadecimal number is odd if it ends with a odd-numbered numeric or letter digit: 1, 3, 5, 7, 9, B, D, F.

Keeping objects unique
One more category of attribute merits further discussion: **Unique Identifiers** (UIDs), with Value Representation UI.

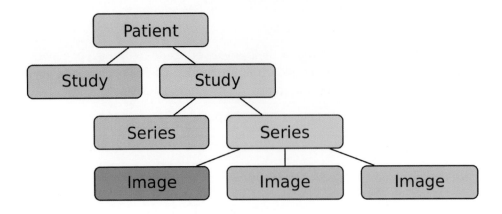

Figure 39: Object Hierarchy

Recall above that a composite IOD includes both the specific IE of interest (in our examples, the image) as well as all the IEs which give it context: in the diagram above, the red image (bottom row) will come packaged up with the pink series, study, and patient IEs from the levels above it in the hierarchy.

This means the same context IEs will be sent numerous times, once for each image: it's essential that these copies are:

- **Consistent**, containing the same values each time they are sent
- **Uniquely identified**, always distinguishable from other objects at the same level or hierarchy

Consistency is enforced with a simple rule: all attributes of a context IE must be the same across all child objects. It's a rather obvious violation of the DICOM standard to send two consecutive slices in the same series but with different patient name attributes.

UIDs
Uniqueness is enforced by defining a single **primary key** at each level of hierarchy. For the patient this is the patient ID, usually a hospital number or an even broader healthcare identifier such as his or her NHS number. For all other levels, a DICOM UID is assigned, with a form like this:

    1.2.826.0.1.1844281.0.52945.31191.20140

UIDs follow very simple rules:

- They can be up to 64 characters long
- They consist only of numeric digits "0-9" and the period "."
- Each group of digits, separated by a period, must be an integer with no leading zeroes (unless it is the number 0)
- Every UID must be globally unique

In theory, global uniqueness is accomplished by registering prefixes to institutions, then appending a further unique suffix for each new object based on some combination of the equipment identifiers, time, and other random or incrementing groups. In practice, many implementations generate UIDs entirely from random or time-based input and rely on the vanishingly small likelihood of collision (and the even smaller likelihood that a colliding UID would ever be shared into the same hospital system).

It can be tempting to "decode" UIDs to extract the date or hospital number often used to construct them. This is a bad idea: any details like this are due to a quirk of the implementation generating that specific UID and shouldn't be relied on. The standard treats them simply as opaque meaningless-but-unique strings.

Class and instance UIDs

DICOM uses UIDs in two ways:

- **Instance UIDs** identify a specific object: for example, a particular study (Mr Smith's MRI on 23 April 2008), series, or image. There are always new, globally-unique values generated within the hospital.
- **Class UIDs** identify the type of an object, they are a concise electronic way of saying "this object conforms to the MR Image IOD defined in the standard". Class UIDs are all defined in the standard or (for private classes) declared in a particular vendor's DICOM documentation.

If you're familiar with object-oriented programming, these terms have the same meaning in DICOM: a *class* is a kind or category of object, and an *instance* is a particular individual object containing actual data.

All the standard DICOM Class UIDs begin with the prefix 1.2.840.10008, and they are all registered in part 6 annex A of the standard. DICOM uses class-style UIDs to represent a number of coded values.

Attribute example: Orientation

We will now examine a specific example of a DICOM attribute of practical use to scientists working in medical imaging. Tomographic image IODs typically include the *Image Plane Module* from part 3 section C.7.2.6, which defines the basic geometric properties of a single slice:

Attribute Name	Tag	Type	Description
Pixel Spacing	(0028,0030)	1	Physical distance in the patient between the centre of each pixel. Specified as adjacent row spacing then adjacent column spacing in mm.
Image Orientation (Patient)	(0020,0037)	1	The direction cosines of the first row and first column with respect to the patient. See C.7.6.2.1.1.
Image Position (Patient)	(0020,0032)	1	The x,y,z co-ordinates of the upper-left corner (centre of the first voxel transmitted) of the image.
Slice Thickness	(0018,0050)	2	Nominal slice thickness in mm.
Slice Location	(0020,1041)	3	Relative position of the plane expressed in mm.

Figure 40: Image Plane Module Attributes

The first three attributes provide enough information to locate every pixel in the 3D co-ordinate system of the patient (of which more below). The fourth and fifth attributes add optional additional information: the measured slice thickness, allowing for gaps or overlap between slices; and a simplified measure of slice position relative to a reference slice.

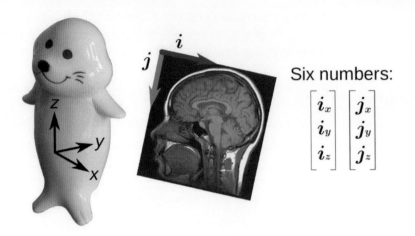

Six numbers:

$$\begin{bmatrix} i_x \\ i_y \\ i_z \end{bmatrix} \begin{bmatrix} j_x \\ j_y \\ j_z \end{bmatrix}$$

Figure 41: DICOM Co-ordinate System

DICOM defines a standard co-ordinate system, in which *x* always increases to the patient's left side, *y* increases towards the patient's back (posterior), and *z* increases towards the patient's head (superior). This is sometimes called a **Left-Posterior-Superior** (LPS) coordinate system.

The *Image Orientation* field is defined in this co-ordinate system. The attribute has a VR of DS (Decimal String), and VM of 6, which is treated as 2 vectors of 3 elements: unit vectors along the row and column directions of the grid of voxels, pointing away from the corner of first voxel in the image. That 'corner voxel' should always be placed in the upper-left corner of the screen when the image is displayed.

Manipulating coordinates
This representation has a number of convenient features. For example, calculating a voxel's position in the patient coordinate system becomes very easy:

$$\begin{bmatrix} x \\ y \\ z \\ 1 \end{bmatrix} = \begin{bmatrix} i_x \cdot \Delta_c & j_x \cdot \Delta_r & 0 & p_x \\ i_y \cdot \Delta_c & j_y \cdot \Delta_r & 0 & p_y \\ i_z \cdot \Delta_c & j_z \cdot \Delta_r & 0 & p_z \\ 0 & 0 & 0 & 1 \end{bmatrix} \begin{bmatrix} m \\ n \\ 0 \\ 1 \end{bmatrix}$$

Figure 42: Voxel Position Calculation

Where *m* and *n* are the indices of the voxel in the image array; Δ_r is the pixel spacing between rows and Δ_c is the pixel spacing between columns from *Pixel Spacing*, *p* is the 3-component vector from *Image Position*, and *i* and *j* are the two 3-component unit vectors from *Image Orientation*.

Standard orientations
Radiology commonly uses three anatomical planes: sagittal, axial, and coronal. Unambiguous representation on-screen is very important.

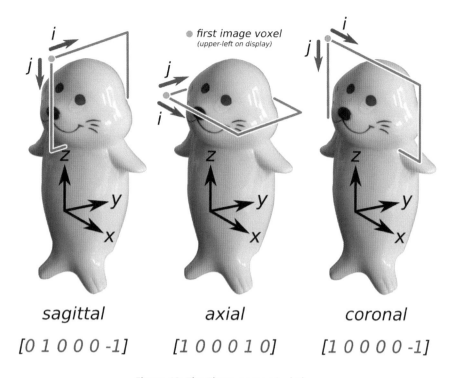

sagittal   axial   coronal

[0 1 0 0 0 -1]   [1 0 0 0 1 0]   [1 0 0 0 0 -1]

Figure 43: The Three Anatomical Planes

This requires the correct **labelling** of axes and the standardisation of **displayed orientation**. Sagittal slices are viewed from the patient's left, in a standing position; coronal in the same position, from the patient's front; and axial slices from the feet, with the patient on their back.

By making the correct choice of corner voxel (which will always be displayed top-left of the screen) and setting the *Image Orientation* vectors shown in the diagram, on-screen display and labelling the standard planes will always be correct.

At the start of this chapter, we noted that a key goal of DICOM is to allow safe operation across big, multi-vendor networks of imaging devices. The orientation attribute is a good example of this. Because of symmetries in the human body, left-right errors are easy to make in medical imaging: in the worst case, these can lead to treatment on the wrong side of the patient's body. By defining a standard, ambiguity-free representation for orientation, DICOM greatly reduces this risk.

DICOM-RT
Another important variant use of DICOM is DICOM-RT, for radiotherapy. All the image types that might go into a radiotherapy planning system (such as CT, PET and MR) are in DICOM format. The metadata for each image type will be slightly different, but that doesn't matter – DICOM means that the planning system can understand the content of the headers and present images to the user in the correct format.

There are 5 main sub-formats of DICOM for radiotherapy: RT structure, RT-Plan, RT-Image, RT-Dose and RT-Treatment record, as summarised below:

DICOM-RT object	Main property	Example contents
RT structure	Patient anatomical information	PTV, OAR, other contours
RT-Plan	Instructions to the linac for patient treatment	Treatment beam details e.g. gantry, collimator and couch angles; jaw and MLC positions.
RT-Image	Radiotherapy image storage/transfer	Simulator, portal image
RT-Dose	Dose distribution data	Patient dose distributions (in 3D), Dose volume histograms
RT-Treatment	Details of treatment delivered to patient	Date and time of treatment, MU delivered, actual linac settings.

Figure 44: Sub-formats of DICOM-RT[59]

They link together as follows:

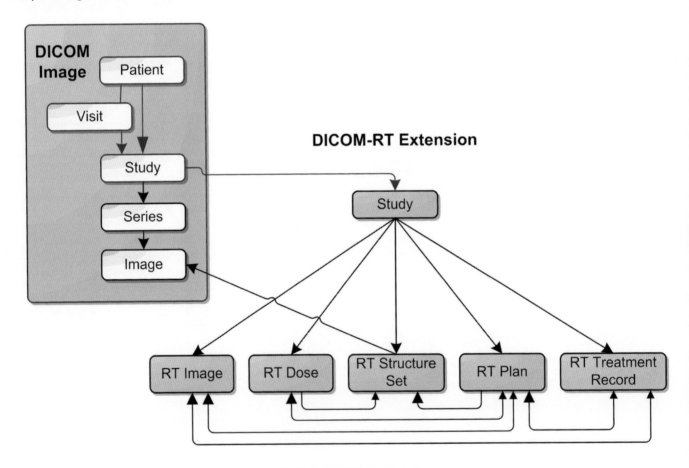

Figure 45: DICOM-RT Objects[60]

This figure shows the DICOM-RT objects as an extension of the DICOM standard. Note that RT Plan, which contains all RT-related information, is an important object that is needed from the start of treatment planning to the completion of treatment and is thus related to all other objects.

They are used in this way: assume we have a set of CT images on a planning system. Once outlines are drawn, usually the target volumes and critical organs, we have a set of contours on which a plan can be designed. This set of contours is stored in the DICOM-RT-Structure set. The patient record now contains a set of DICOM images and a DICOM-RT-Structure set, which contains details on the number of contours drawn, number of points in each contour and their names. This set defines a set of areas of significance, such as body contours, tumour volumes (e.g. gross target volume, clinical target volume, planning target volume), OARs, and other regions of interest.

Next some beams are added to the plan, which generates the RT-Plan, which contains details of each treatment beam, such as its name, jaw settings, energy, monitor units etc. In the DICOM-RT standard, information about the structures of interest is contained in DICOM-RT-Structure set and dose distribution in the DICOM-RT RT-Dose file, which requires the coordinates for placing their positions in relation to each other. Thus, the RT-Plan object refers only to the textual information in treatment plans, whether generated manually or by a treatment planning system.

A dose calculation is now done and this generates the DICOM-RT RT-Dose file, which contains details of the dose calculation matrix geometry, dose volume histogram etc.

Digitally reconstructed radiographs may be produced during the planning and placed in the DICOM-RT RT-Image file. Verification images taken using an electronic portal imaging device also generate images in RT-Image format. Note that CT images generated with CT simulators are considered to be ordinary CT scans and do not use the RT-extensions. In contrast to a DICOM image object, RT Image includes not only image information, but also the presentation of the image (i.e. the position, plane and orientation of the image and the distance from the machine source to the imaging plane). The RT-Image file may (if necessary) include the table position, isocentre position and patient position, together with the type of device used to limit the radiotherapy beam (e.g. a multi-leaf collimator).

Once the plan is ready for treatment, some or all of these files may be sent to the linac control system. The RT-Plan is essential in this respect but some of the others are optional and the functionality available may be vendor specific. Every time the patient has treatment, the treatment parameters used are stored by the record and verify system and at the end of treatment the full treatment record is stored in the DICOM-RT RT-Treatment file.

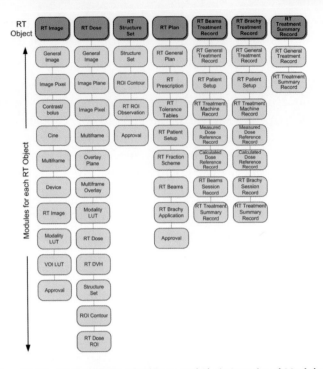

Figure 46: The Seven DICOM-RT Objects and Their Associated Modules[61].

One often overlooked benefit of such standardisation is in upgrading and replacing systems: a new system is far more likely to be able to read old data, hence data retention can be achieved without having to keep a sample of the old system just in case the old data needs to be accessed.

Chapter 6 – Software Development

Software engineering

Software engineering is the application of engineering to the design, development, implementation, testing and maintenance of software in a systematic method.

Typical formal definitions of software engineering are:

"*the systematic application of scientific and technological knowledge, methods, and experience to the design, implementation, testing, and documentation of software*"[62];

"*the application of a systematic, disciplined, quantifiable approach to the development, operation, and maintenance of software*"; ("IEEE Standard Glossary of Software Engineering Terminology," IEEE std 610.12-1990, 1990.)

"*an engineering discipline that is concerned with all aspects of software production*"[63];

"*the establishment and use of sound engineering principles in order to economically obtain software that is reliable and works efficiently on real machines.*" [64]

All of which say that it's the application of engineering principles to the development of software. The 1996 "Dictionary of Computing[65]" says that software engineering is the entire range of activities used to design and develop software, with some connotation of "good practice". It then lists a whole range of activities:

- User requirements elicitation
- Software requirements definition
- Architectural and detailed design
- Program specification
- Program development using some recognised approach such as structured programming
- Systematic testing techniques
- Program correctness proofs
- Software quality assurance
- Software project management
- Documentation
- Performance and timing analysis
- Development and use of software engineering environments.

Software engineering is expected to address the practical problems of software development, including those encountered with large or complex systems. It is thus a mix of formal and pragmatic techniques.

Introduction to programming

There isn't enough room in this book to completely describe the art of Computer Programming – indeed, Donald Knuth devoted several large volumes to it[66][i]. What we will consider here are instead those elements of software coding that are to be found in most high-level (and in some cases low-level) languages, with examples from various languages. These elements might be considered as building-blocks. But how do we know which ones we need for the thing that we're planning to build?

We will look at a technique called "structured programming" (also known as "top-down programming" or "stepwise refinement"). It is a software development technique that imposes a hierarchical structure on the design of the program. It starts out by defining the solution at the highest level of functionality and breaking it down further and

---

[i] His planned 7-volume opus on the topic saw the first 3 published in 1968-1973 with volume 4A appearing in 2011 and 4B is expected to appear in sections from 2019 onwards.

further into small routines that can be easily documented and coded. As an example, we'll look at reading in a set of numbers from a file, sorting them, and writing them back out again to another file.

First we need to look at how we're going to sort them and we'll use bubblesort, generally viewed as the simplest of the efficient methods. Bubblesort repeatedly works its way through a list, comparing items in pairs and swapping them if they're in the wrong order.

Structured programming is an iterative approach, in that it takes the output from one step as the input to the next. So in step 1 we identify the major modules. In our example they are: Read from a file; Sort (using bubblesort); Write to a file.

Step 2 is to break each major module down into smaller modules, so for the "read from file" module we may write:

- Ask the user for the name of the file to read from
- Open the file
- Read the numbers in the file
- Close the file

Then we repeat it again, so for "Read the numbers in the file" we break it down into:

```
While there are numbers to be read
{
        Read the next number
}
```

Note the use of the curly brackets to enclose a group of commands (even though there's only one in this example) that is controlled by the statement just before the open bracket ("While" in this case).

If we apply this technique to the bubblesort itself, we get:

```
For as many times as there are numbers
{
        For each pair of numbers
        {
                if they are in the wrong order
                {
                        Swap them
                }
        }
}
```

Again note the use of the curly brackets to enclose blocks – in these examples there is only one statement in each block, but there could be multiples. Note also the "blocks within blocks" and the use of indentation to easily see where a block starts and ends – a useful way of spotting when a closing bracket has been omitted.

It should also be noted that this is a very good example of pseudocode – it has no language-dependent lines, saying what is to be done but not how to do it.

The basic principle of structured programming is therefore: If something is complex/difficult, break it down into easier pieces. This is often known as "Problem decomposition" and is common in most maths-based science.

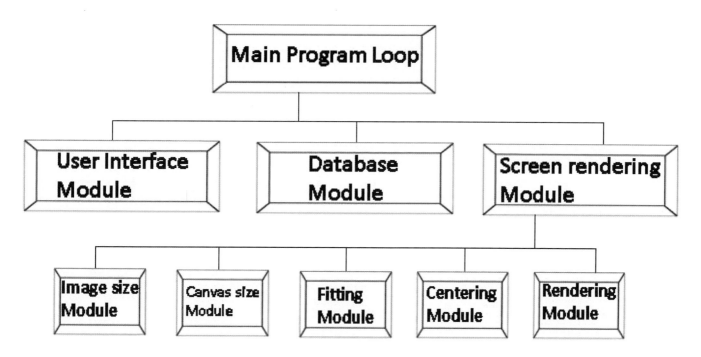

Figure 47: Top down design example

In comparison, bottom-up design works the other way around: it defines the modules and then builds them up into a complete system. This approach can be very helpful where libraries of code are to be utilised, especially those interfacing with hardware. New base-level functionality cannot be constructed, so the system has to be built from what is available. Bottom-up may also be a better way of handling constraints within a specification.

We've picked up three of the most important elements in programming in the blocks above: *while* something is true, *for* a specific number of times and *if* something is true. We need one more fundamental element before we can do any actual programming, though: storage.

Let's look again at the line at the heart of bubblesort: "Swap them". If we're dealing with numbers, then we need to have stored them somewhere, so we can recall them and compare them.

The first thing any program requires therefore is somewhere to store values. The base types are straightforward (integers, text, booleans[ii]) but from these bases more complex types can be built. Some languages require this storage[iii] to be declared prior to use (e.g. C), whereas others (e.g. Python) allow declaration at use.

The naming of variables may be prescribed by the language (e.g. in some forms of BASIC a variable ending in "$" is of type text; in FORTRAN variables whose names start with a letter between I and N are integers; in M (formerly MUMPS) variables prefixed with "^" indicate disc or permanent storage). The most common form of variable naming is what is known as "Hungarian notation" where the variable name (starting with a capital letter) is prefixed with one or more lower case letters that denotes its type, e.g. nRank is numeric, sName is string (text) and bCapsLockOn is boolean.

Hungarian notation is named after Charles Simonyi, a Hungarian employee at Microsoft who developed it. Hungarian names are, unusually for Europe, rendered surname first. Thus Hungarian notation renders the variable name with the type ("n") first, followed by the unique name ("Rank") to make the full name of the variable

---

[ii] Booleans store values that are either TRUE or FALSE
[iii] Often termed "variables"

("nRank")[iv]. This simple example also demonstrates its use as "nRank" may contain a positional index whereas "sRank" may contain a military title. As with many things in programming conventions, you only really start to realise how useful they are when you come back to a huge program which you wrote five years ago and now need to make some changes to. I have programs for which I spent ages building the infrastructure correctly and setting everything up correctly. When I need to make a change to them, it's easy: the code just flows and corrections and improvements are simple and effective. I also have others which I wrote in a hurry, so didn't build the right infrastructure and when I want to make changes to them I have to follow lots of code through to make sure that the changes I'm about to make aren't going to break something else. I therefore end up retro-fitting the infrastructure in order to better understand what I'm doing and improve my life in the future. The worst mistake you can make in programming is to assume that you will never need to change the code.

Assigning a value to a variable (i.e. storing the value in the named location) is usually done via the '=' operator, but more complex data types may have their own method.

All languages contain key words which are part of it and form instructions. These are called "reserved words" and cannot be used as variable names (although they can be used as part of a name, e.g. "If" is a reserved word so cannot be used as a variable name, whereas "IfPrinting" is an acceptable name[v]).

The control blocks we saw earlier are what gives software its intelligence. They determine the flow of the processing, so we will now examine some examples in specific languages. We've already met "if", which in Visual Basic (VB) is rendered:

```
If nMonth=9 or nMonth=4 or nMonth=6 or nMonth=11 Then
        nDays=30
ElseIf nMonth<>2 Then
        nDays=31
Else
        nDays=28
End If
```

Note the use of "End If" to close the control block, otherwise the program doesn't know whether the next statement is part of the final "Else" or not[vi].

[iv] There are those that dislike Hungarian notation, feeling that it can obscure code and is only alerting you to errors that the compiler should pick up anyway. However, in non-declarative languages such as Python, the compiler will not provide this assistance and so Hungarian Notation is to be preferred. See https://www.joelonsoftware.com/2005/05/11/making-wrong-code-look-wrong/ for an interesting discussion.

[v] Although bIfPrinting would be better

[vi] None of these code samples handle leap years – that is left for the reader to implement

Another decision-making structure is the *switch*, which in C (for the same example) would be:

```
switch(nMonth)
{
        case 9:
        case 4:
        case 6:
        case 11:
                nDays=30;
                break;
        case 2:
                nDays=28;
                break;
        default:
                nDays=31;
                break;
}
```

Note the use of "break" to indicate that processing should continue after the switch clause. It is therefore superfluous in the final "default" clause and doesn't aid readability – however it is good practice as other "case" clauses can be added after it and it may thus prevent erroneous processing. Note the use of ';' to indicate the end of a line of code – this allows statements to be broken up when writing, say over several lines, in order to improve readability. It does lead to the most annoying C error message of "missing semi-colon", though.

Having done decisions, the other type of control block is repetition, of which our example contains two. Firstly, *for*, which in JavaScript to output a list of powers of 2 looks like:

```
n=1;
for (i=0; i<10; i++)
{
        document.write("2^" + i + " = " + n + ", ");
        n=n*2;
}
```

And finally *while*, which might be used in a C program to output powers of 2 that are less than 1 million as follows[vii]:

```
n=1;
i=0;
while (n<1000000)
{
        n*=2;
        i++;
        cout << "2^" << i << " = " << n << ", ";
}
```

[vii] Actually, it doesn't. It goes to one more, as n is over one million when the *while* test fails and the loop terminates

The final item a language requires is a mechanism for input and output. In VB this is achieved through statements such as:

```
FileOpen(1, "PATIENTLIST", OpenMode.Input)
Input(1, sPatName)
Debug.WriteLine(sPatName)
```

Some languages use the same statements to input from the user as to input from a file, and to output to a file as to output to screen or printer. Whilst this aids the speed of learning the language, it does not assist code readability.

All of the above aid the development of computer programs, but the common feature (sadly probably the least used) which greatly aids the maintenance of code is the comment. This is a piece of text which is ignored by the compiler/interpreter and plays no part whatsoever in the execution of the program. It does, however, carry information. There have been many attempts to codify the use of comments, from the simple "one comment every 10 lines of code" (resulting in useless comments such as "this is a comment" and failing to document more complex coding), to a more complex rigidly-defined comment block at the head of every subroutine describing variables used, the execution path and all revisions to the code since it was originally authored.

An example for one of the routines above might be, in C:

```
/* *******************************************
Routine to calculate number of days in a month
Written: Paul Ganney, 10/5/85
Edit[viii]: Paul Ganney, 11/2/88 correction for leap years
Edit: Paul Ganney, 5/1/00 correction for 2000 not being a leap year

Inputs:
nMonth: month number (Jan=1, Dec=12)
nYear: year number as 4 digits

Outputs:
nDays: number of days in month

Execution: simple switch statement
*/
```

Note the use of /* and */ to denote the start and end of a comment block.

The most prevalent use of comments is probably as an aide-memoire to the programmer: a line of code that required the author to have to think carefully about when writing certainly requires a comment so that the logic behind it need not be recreated every time the code is altered. This though, is insufficient when multiple programmers are working on a system at the same time and a solid commenting methodology should form part of the design. There are two useful rules of thumb: "you cannot have too many comments" and "there are not enough comments yet". An example of such an aide-memoire (again in C) might be:

```
nCurrentItem=pDoc->NextPage(nCurrentItem-1)+1;  // nCurrentItem-1 is the one currently on screen
```

Note the different comment: it starts with // and ends at the end of the line.

[viii] The edit that should have appeared in the previous code examples

Subroutines are not only good practice for placing the same code into one place (so maintenance is easier) but they also aid documentation: consider the code required for the subroutine in the example above (which we met whilst discussing the if statement), compared to

nDays=DaysInMonth(nCurrentMonth);

which is quicker and easier to read each time the code is encountered.

One approach to writing code is to first write pseudocode, which describes the logic/action to be performed but in a human-readable form (see the bubblesort example earlier). Converting this into comments means that the logic is preserved when the pseudocode is converted into actual code.

And don't forget that the comments will only be read by humans – one of the joys of the lunar lander code being released was the sense of humour of the engineers, so do feel free to fill them with the occasional joke.

if(MakeLower(sInput)==MakeLower(sPassword)) // CAPS LOCK – Preventing Login Since 1980

Version Control

As with any document, version control is vital in software development. There are two elements to this:

- Ensuring developers are all working on the latest version of the code.
- Ensuring users are all executing the latest version of the code.

There are multiple ways (and multiple products) to achieve this, so we will examine only one example of each.

Developers: A common code repository enables multi-programmer projects to be successfully developed. This repository allows all developers access to all the code for reading. When a developer wishes to work on a piece of code, this is "checked out" and no other developer may then access the code for alteration until it is "checked in" again. Dependency analysis is then utilised to alert all developers to other code modules which depend upon the altered code and may therefore require revision or re-validation.

Probably the most popular code repository is git (or github) possibly because it is free open-source software distributed under the terms of the GNU General Public License version 2. Git is a distributed version-control system for tracking changes in source code during software development. While it was designed for coordinating work among programmers, it can actually be used to track changes in any set of files as it is not code-sensitive. Its goals include speed, data integrity and support for distributed, non-linear workflows. Git was originally created by Linus Torvalds[ix] in 2005 for development of the Linux kernel. This is a snapshot-based repository in that a commit takes a snapshot of the code at that point, unlike other systems (such as Subversion) which record a set of file-based changes. To avoid inefficiency, git doesn't re-store unchanged files, merely a pointer to any such. Git therefore only ever adds data – a deletion still needs the old file to be stored so that deletion can be rolled back. Git has three main states that files can reside in: committed, modified, and staged. Committed files are stored in the local database. Modified files have been changed but have not yet been committed to the database. Staged files are modified files marked to go into the next commit snapshot in this current version. The git workflow is therefore:

- Files in the working directory are modified.
- These files are staged, adding snapshots of them to the staging area.
- A commit is performed, which takes the files as they are in the staging area and stores that snapshot permanently to the Git directory.

Users: In a database project (or any software that accesses a database, regardless of whether that is its core functionality[x]) it is possible to ensure that all users are using the latest version of the software by hard-coding the

---

[ix] Torvalds said: "I'm an egotistical bastard, and I name all my projects after myself. First 'Linux', now 'git'." (PC World. 14 July 2012)
[x] It is worth remembering that a password list is a simple database

version into the source code and checking it against the version in the database. If the database has a later version number, then the program can alert the user, advising them to upgrade or even halting their progress (depending on the nature of the upgrade).

Chapter 7 – Software Lifecycle

The lifecycle of a software system runs from the identification of a requirement until it is phased out, perhaps to be replaced by another system. It defines the stages of software development and the order in which these stages are executed. The basic building blocks of all software lifecycle models include:

1. Gathering and analysing user requirements
2. Software design
3. Coding
4. Testing
5. Installation & maintenance

Each phase produces deliverables required by the next stage in the lifecycle. These requirements are translated into design and code is produced driven by the design. Testing then verifies the deliverable of the coding stage against the requirements. This tested software is installed and maintained for its lifespan. Maintenance requests may involve additions or revisions to the requirements and the cycle then repeats.

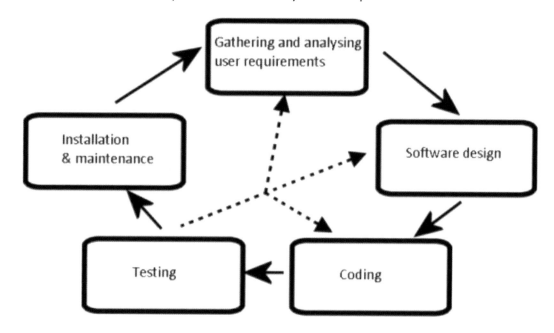

Figure 48: The Stages in a Software Lifecycle

If testing reveals errors, then the process may return to any one of the three preceding stages. Release would normally come between the "Test" and "Maintain" stages

Requirements Specification

This phase of the lifecycle identifies the problem to be solved and maps out in detail what the user requires. The problem may be to automate a user task, to improve efficiency or productivity within a user group, to correct shortcomings of existing software, to control a device, etc. Requirements on software are usually a complex combination of requirements from a variety of users associated with a problem. Requirements specification may therefore also include systems analysis meaning that this stage may range from simply taking notes during a meeting to needing to interview and observe a wide range of users and processes.

Software Design

Software design typically involves two levels of design – namely architectural and detailed design. The architectural design specifies the basic components of the software system such as the user interface, database, reporting module, etc. often using tools such as **Data Flow Diagrams** (DFD) and **Entity-Relation Diagrams** (ERD). Detailed design elaborates on each of these components in terms of tables and fields in the database, layout and data to be displayed on the graphical user interface, and often pseudo-code for any data analysis modules. In the example in Figure 49, a customer will place an order, using the product options, which will trigger the subsequent events (generate invoice etc.). The chain of triggered events will eventually terminate at a responsible actor, such as the factory. Note that the customer appears twice – once as initiator and once as receiver.

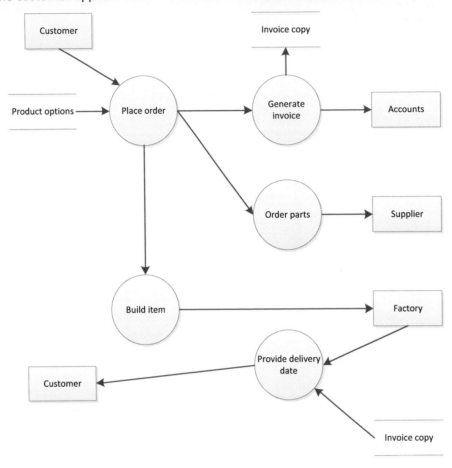

Figure 49: A Data Flow Diagram for an Ordering System

Software Development and Coding
This phase of the software development lifecycle converts the design into a complete software package. It brings together the hardware, software and communications elements for the system. It is often driven by the detailed design phase and must take into consideration practical issues in terms of resource availability, feasibility and technological constraints. Choice of development platform is often constrained by availability of skills, software and hardware. A compromise must be found between the resources available and the ability to meet software requirements. A good programmer rarely blames the platform for problems with the software.

Software Testing
Software testing is an ongoing process along the development to maintenance path. There are 3 main levels of testing:

1. Unit testing: individual modules are tested against set criteria.
2. Integration testing: the relationships between modules are tested.
3. System testing: the workings of the software system as a whole are tested.

Test criteria should include functionality, usability, performance and adherence to standards. Test cases are usually generated during the design stage for each level of testing. These may be added to or modified along the pathway but should, at least, cover the basic criteria. Testing objectives also influence the set of test cases. For example, the test cases for acceptance testing might differ from those for a beta test or even a usability test.

There are many ways of testing software and these are very closely linked to validation and verification. The primary purpose of validation and verification (when applied to medical software) is safety. Functionality is a secondary purpose, although without functionality the code is pointless. The way to reconcile this is to consider the consequences of a failure of the code: a system that is 75% functional but 100% safe is still usable (albeit annoying) – if the figures are reversed, it is not.

In validating and verifying a system as safe, one starts from the premise that all software contains "bugs". These "bugs" may be classified as faults, errors or failures.

A fault is a mistake in the design or code, which may lead to an error (but equally may not), such as declaring an array to be the wrong size. An error is unspecified behaviour in execution, which may lead to a failure, such as messages starting with non-numeric codes being discarded as they evaluate to zero. A failure is the crossing of a safety threshold due to an uncontained error.

There are two main approaches to testing, often referred to as "black box" and "white box". Applying this to software testing, the "box" is the program, or module, that is to be tested.

In black box testing, the contents of the box are unknown[i]. Therefore, tests comprise of a known set of inputs and the predetermined output that this should provide. This is very useful when the software has been commissioned using an **Output-Based Specification** (OBS) or for end-user testing. It also removes any effect that may be caused by the application of the debugger environment itself[ii].

In white-box testing (also known as clear box, glass box or transparent box testing, which may be a better descriptor of the process) the contents of the box are known and are exposed. In software terms, this may mean that the source code is available or even that the code is being tested in the development environment via single-stepping. It is therefore usually applied to structures or elements of a software system, rather than to its whole. It is also not unusual for a black box failure to be investigated using white box testing.

In generic terms, therefore, black box testing is functional testing whereas white box testing is structural or unit testing. Thus a large system comprising multiple components will often have each component white box tested and the overall system black box tested in order to test the integration and interfacing of the components. In upgrading a software system, it will be black-box testing that is undertaken as the code will not be available.

Testing should normally be undertaken by someone different to the software author. A draft BCS standard (2001)[67] lists the following increasing degrees of independence:

a) the test cases are designed by the person(s) who writes the component under test;
b) the test cases are designed by another person(s);
c) the test cases are designed by a person(s) from a different section;
d) the test cases are designed by a person(s) from a different organisation;
e) the test cases are not chosen by a person.

There are multiple test case design techniques with corresponding test measurement techniques.

The following non-exhaustive list is based on ISO 29119-4 "Software and systems engineering - Software testing - Part 4: Test techniques" [68]. Not all will be required or applicable for each project.

---

[i] But not in a Schrodinger sense.
[ii] It is extremely annoying to find that code runs perfectly under the debugger but not outside of it.

- Specification-based test design techniques (Black Box)
  - Equivalence partitioning
  - Classification tree method
  - Boundary-value analysis
  - Syntax testing
  - Decision table testing
  - Cause-effect graphing
  - State transition testing
  - Scenario testing
  - Random testing
- Structure-based test design techniques (White box)
  - Statement testing
  - Branch testing
  - Decision testing
  - Modified Condition Decision Coverage (MCDC) testing
  - Data flow testing
  - Experience-based test design techniques
- Error guessing

It is instructive to examine one of these, together with its corresponding measurement technique. The one we will select is Boundary Value Analysis. This takes the specification of the component's behaviour and collates a set of input and output values (both valid and invalid). These input and output values are then partitioned into a number of ordered sets with identifiable boundaries. This is done by grouping together the input and output values which are expected to be treated by the component in the same way: thus they are considered equivalent due to the equivalence of the component's behaviour. The boundaries of each partition are normally the values of the boundaries between partitions, but where partitions are disjoint the minimum and maximum values within the partition are used. The boundaries of both valid and invalid partitions are used.

The rationale behind this method of testing is the premise that the inputs and outputs of a component can be partitioned into classes that will be treated similarly by the component and, secondly, that developers are prone to making errors at the boundaries of these classes.

For example, a program to calculate factorials

This program would have the partitions (assuming integer input only):

- Partition a: $-\infty$ to 0 (not defined)
- Partition b: 1 to n (where n! is the largest integer the component can handle, so for a standard C integer with a maximum value of 2147483647, n would be 12)
- Partition c: n+1 to $+\infty$ (unable to be handled)

The boundary values are therefore 0, 1, n and n+1. The test cases that are used are three per boundary: the boundary values and ones an incremental distance to either side. Duplicates are then removed, giving a test set in our example of {-1, 0, 1, 2, n-1, n, n+1, n+2}. Each value produces a test case comprising the input value, the boundary tested and the expected outcome. Additional test cases may be designed to ensure invalid output values cannot be induced. Note that invalid as well as valid input values are used for testing.

It can clearly be seen that this technique is only applicable for black-box testing.

The corresponding measurement technique (Boundary Value Coverage) defines the coverage items as the boundaries of the partitions. Some partitions may not have an identified boundary, as in our example where Partition a has no lower bound and Partition c no upper bound. Coverage is calculated as follows:

$$BoundaryValueCoverage = \frac{number\ of\ distinct\ boundary\ values\ executed}{total\ number\ of\ boundary\ values}.100\%$$

In our example, the coverage is 100% as all identified boundaries are exercised by at least one test case (although +∞ and -∞ were listed as the limits of partitions c and a, they are not boundaries as they indicate the partitions are unbounded). Lower levels of coverage would be achieved if all the boundaries we had identified were not all exercised, or could not be (for example, if 2147483647 was required to be tested, where 2147483648 is too large to be stored). If all the boundaries are not identified, then any coverage measure based on this incomplete set of boundaries would be misleading.[iii]

Software Maintenance

Software maintenance is defined in the IEEE Standard for Software Maintenance[iv] as *"the modification of a software product after delivery to correct faults, to improve performance or other attributes, or to adapt the product to a modified environment"*. It lasts for the lifespan of the software and requires careful logging and tracking of change requests as per the guidelines for change management set out at the end of the requirements phase.

A maintenance request often goes through a lifecycle similar to software development. The request is analysed, its impact on the system as a whole determined and any required modifications are designed, coded, tested and finally implemented. Training and day-to-day support are also core components of the software maintenance phase. It is therefore essential for the maintainer to be able to understand the existing code[v]. Good documentation and clear and simple coding at the development stage will be most helpful at this point especially if the developer is not available or if there has been a long time gap since development.

There are many tools that provide help with the discipline of software development, such as, in Unix/Linux, SVN[vi] and 'make', which codifies instructions for compiling and linking. Document management systems such as OSS wiki and Q-Pulse[69] can help departments log their activities, including the queries that are raised during the complete software lifecycle.

Software Lifecycle Models

The software lifecycle models help to manage the software development process from conception through to implementation within time and cost constraints. We consider four such here.

Waterfall Model

The Waterfall methodology (also known as a linear-sequential model) forms the heart of all other development methodologies, so it is worth examining first. It is also very simple to understand and use and follows a structured sequential path from requirements to maintenance. It sets out milestones at each stage which must be accomplished before the next stage can begin.

The waterfall methodology follows a simple idea: each part of the process forms a complete unit and progress only passes to the next unit once its predecessor is complete. There is clearly a great alignment with the PRINCE 2[70] project management technique (for "unit" read "stage" and it becomes very clear, so we will use this terminology from now on) which is probably why, despite being much maligned, Waterfall is still in very common use today. It is also very simple to understand (and therefore simple to explain to non-technical members of a project team or board) and transfers easily into milestones and deliverables which can be measured.

[iii] A fuller worked example can be found at http://www.testingstandards.co.uk/Component%20Testing.pdf
[iv] Originally 1219-1998 but superseded by 14764:2006
[v] Which brings us back to the art of comments
[vi] Apache Subversion

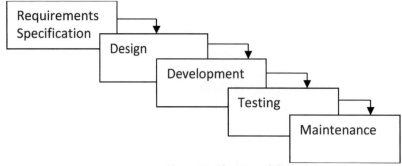

Figure 50: The Waterfall Model

The rigidity of the Waterfall model aids project management with well-defined milestones and deliverables. It does however restrict flexibility and does not provide much scope for user feedback until software development has been completed. It is only suitable for small-scale projects where user requirements are clearly defined and unlikely to change over the software lifespan.

The major flaw of a Waterfall model is that there is no way to return to an earlier stage. In other words, features that have been omitted from the design cannot be added in: the final product is exactly what was specified, whether or not that is now what is required. New features may be added post-implementation, but that is a project in itself which will follow the same lifecycle model.

Incremental Model/Prototyping Model

The incremental model is an intuitive amendment to the waterfall model. In this model, there are multiple iterations of smaller cycles involving the key stages of formalised requirements, design, development, and testing. Each cycle produces a prototype of the software. Subsequent iterations thus improve or build on the previous prototype.

This approach is more suited to the small scale development often experienced by Physics and Engineering Departments but only really works if it is properly controlled. It is essential that both the disadvantages and advantages of this approach are understood before commencing a project using such a methodology (and especially before deciding against the Spiral method which we will cover in the next section).

The obvious advantage that this methodology gives is that requirements that are difficult to completely define in advance of development commencing can progress through several prototypes, assisting the user in planning the final software's use and it can help to determine the full requirements for the system. It is also an effective method to demonstrate the feasibility of a certain approach for novel systems where it is not clear whether constraints can be met or whether algorithms can be developed to implement the requirements. Testing and code management is simpler with smaller cycles and errors can be detected early, allowing them to be corrected by re-design rather than by patches. As users have a tendency to change their minds in specifying requirements once they have seen the software, this method of developing systems allows team-development.

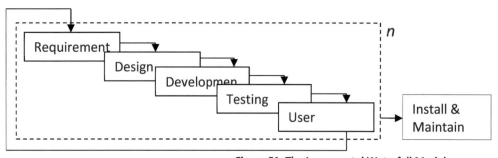

Figure 51: The Incremental Waterfall Model

The major problems with incremental models are the "scope creep" that can often result from frequent user feedback incrementally increasing the requirements at each iteration and also the associated risk of getting stuck in a never-ending development loop with no final product being released. Another potential problem is that, as the requirements for the entire system are not gathered at the start of the project, the system architecture might be affected at later iterations: the initial design (especially the software infrastructure such as entities and classes) may not be the optimal one for the final product. This introduces the risk of a build-and-patch approach through development, leading to poor code design and increasing the complexity of testing.

Spiral Model

The Spiral Model was designed to include the best features from the Waterfall and Prototyping Models. It is similar to the incremental model, but at the end of each iteration (called a spiral in this model) a robust working version of the software is released for user evaluation. This release will not be complete in functionality, but – having completed testing – will be safe. Users are thus able to work with the software (albeit in a reduced capacity) early in the development cycle, which can alleviate some of the constraints around development time.

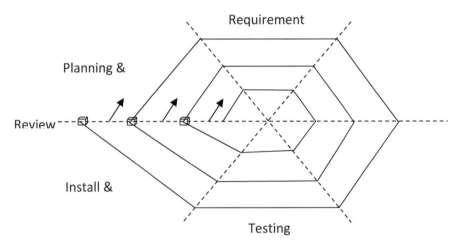

Figure 52: The Spiral Model

The development of each version of the system is carefully designed using the steps involved in the Waterfall Model. The first version is called the 'baseline spiral' and each subsequent spiral builds on the baseline spiral, each producing a new version with increased functionality. The theory is that the set of requirements is hierarchical in nature, with additional functionality building on each preceding release. The spiral model specifies risk analysis and management explicitly which helps to keep the software development process under control. This is a good model for systems where the entire problem is well defined from the start, such as modelling and simulation software, but not so much for database projects where most functions are essentially independent.

Agile Methodology

Web-based software and mobile applications have led to a requirement for quick releases and less focus on the traditional requirements→design→development process. The Agile methodology stresses collaboration over documentation and constant evolution over detailed design.

Agile software development is a set of frameworks and practices based on the Agile Manifesto[vii] that provides guidance on how to adapt and respond quickly to requirement changes in a constantly evolving environment.

Popular Agile frameworks include Scrum and Kanban. An agile software development process always starts by defining the users and the vision for the problem to be solved. The problem is then further sub-divided into user

---

[vii] https://agilemanifesto.org/

stories which are prioritised and delivered in chunks at regular intervals called sprints. Each sprint delivers a releasable product increment.

The main difference between the agile methodology and the three previously described is a change in mindset. Unlike the waterfall model where a solution to the entire problem is considered at the outset, Agile aims to look at specific use cases or user stories at a time and develop and test those with users. This provides the ability to change tracks quickly when requirements change.

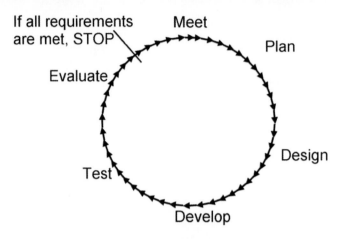

Figure 53: The Agile Model

The models discussed here are some of the basic models and individual software projects may sometimes combine techniques from different models to suit their specific needs. Medical Physics/Clinical Engineering projects often follow an iterative approach since the requirements are not always clearly defined and they may undergo frequent revisions. It is essential in such cases to maintain a robust software change control process (which leads nicely into "Software Quality Assurance", next) and to document **Corrective And Preventative Actions** (CAPA), as no software is ever perfect, bug-free or finished, therefore.

So why use one[71]? A 2015 study by the Standish Group across 50,000 software projects discovered that:

- Only 29% of projects were completely successful
- 52% had major challenges
- 19% failed completely

For these reasons:

1. The wrong development partner/team
2. The wrong development model. (Agile vs. Waterfall)
3. Poor understanding of software development.
4. Unrealistic/risky goals for development.
5. Wrong expectations set by developer.

It has been argued (e.g. by the blog that furnished this information) that Agile is far superior to Waterfall for reasons such as:

- Speed-to-market: it is estimated that about 80% of all market leaders were first to market. Agile development philosophy supports the notion of early and regular releases, and 'perpetual beta'.
- Quality: A key principle of agile development is that testing is integrated throughout the lifecycle, enabling regular inspection of the working product as it develops.
- Business Engagement/Customer Satisfaction: Agile development principles encourage active 'user' involvement throughout the product's development and a very cooperative collaborative approach.

- Risk Management: Small incremental releases made visible to the product owner and product team through its development help to identify any issues early and make it easier to respond to change or to rollback to an earlier version.
- Cost Control: An Agile approach of fixed timescales and evolving requirements enables a fixed budget so that the scope of the product and its features are variable, rather than the cost.
- Right Product: Agile development requirements emerge and evolve, and the ability to embrace change (with the appropriate trade-offs) enables the team to build the right product.
- More Enjoyable: debatable, especially for the project manager.

Software Quality Assurance

The terms "**Software Quality Assurance**" (SQA) and "**Software Quality Control**" (SQC) are often mistakenly used interchangeably. The definition offered by the now defunct website[viii] sqa.net is:

> "Software Quality Assurance [is] the function of software quality that assures that the standards, processes and procedures are appropriate for the project and are correctly implemented.

> Software Quality Control [is] the function of software quality that checks that the project follows its standards processes, and procedures, and that the project produces the required internal and external (deliverable) products."

The two components can thus be seen as one (SQA) setting the standards that are to be followed with the other (SQC) ensuring that they have been. The process for SQC is one that should be specified as part of SQA so that the method for measurement and thus the criteria for compliance are known up-front. For example, the SQA may specify that ISO 14915 be used to define the multi-media user interfaces. SQC will therefore test to ensure that all multi-media user interfaces comply. It is thus clear that SQC will be undertaking a level of testing and it is not unusual for the full test suite to be part of the SQC process – testing not just the standards employed, but the functionality and safety of the software also.

It is common to break the software down into attributes that can be measured and in this there is a similarity with software testing (already covered). There are several definitions of software quality attributes: McCall (1977), Boehm (1978), Robert Grady's FURPS[72][ix]+ and Microsoft's Common Quality Attributes[73].

[viii] It existed in 2020 but is no more. The definitions are oft-quoted, with one source attributing them to NASA (although they're not on NASA's website either). They're good definitions though.

[ix] Functionality, Usability, Reliability, Performance, Supportability, constraints (such as design, implementation, interface and physical).

Some such attributes are:

- Accuracy – the ability of the system to produce accurate results (and to what level of accuracy this is required).
- Availability – the proportion of time that the system is functional and working.
- Compatibility – the ability of the system to work with, for example, different input devices.
- Functionality – what the system is actually supposed to do.
- Manageability – the ease with which system administrators can manage the system, through tuning, debugging and monitoring.
- Performance – the responsiveness of a system to execute a required action with a set time frame.
- Security – the ability of a system to resist malicious interference (covered in "security" on page 118).
- Supportability – the ability of the system to provide information to assist in rectifying a performance failure.
- Usability – how well the system meets the users' requirements by being intuitive and accessible. (Standards may seem limiting and anti-creative, but Microsoft's success is built on them, especially the common Windows user interface[x].)

Three further areas fall into the remit of SQA, all of which assume that the system (and especially the software at the heart of it) will not remain constant over time (it is often said that software is never finished, only implemented and passed to users): Configuration Management, Change Control and Documentation, which we will now examine.

Software Configuration Management (SCM) is the tracking and controlling of changes in the software. It therefore requires a robust **Change Control** (CC) method. The TickIT guide[74] has two quality control elements covering this: "Maintain and Enhance" and "Support", listing the following control mechanisms:

- Change control approval points: authority to proceed with change
- Full release approval
- Regression tests
- System, integration and acceptance test
- Reviews and audits
- Configuration and change management
- Quality plans and projects plans

It can therefore be seen that changes to a live system should not be undertaken lightly. They require possibly more consideration than the initial system to ensure that a fix doesn't cause more problems[xi]. A risk assessment, covering both the risk of making the change as well as the risk of not doing so, must be undertaken. Requiring authorisation ensures that SQA is undertaken. If you compare this with the hazard logs discussed earlier, then the major addition is the "do nothing" risk.

Like the software, the documentation must be kept up to date. It must form an accurate reflection of the software in use and should thus undertake the same version control as the software (discussed on page 77) at the same time. It is therefore clear that the system documentation (in several parts: user guide, programmers' guide, system administrators' guide, etc.) must have a clear structure to it. Without such structure, the documentation becomes difficult to maintain.

In order to enable programmers to work across multiple projects employing several languages, it is vital that the documentation has a consistent format to it so that information can be swiftly found and easily updated. In other words, the documentation also requires a standard, which should be part of the SQA process that it also enables.

---

[x] left-click to select, right-click for a context menu, commonality of icons so "save" always looks the same, etc.
[xi] An IT director once told me that his aim for his support staff was that they fixed more problems than they caused. Sadly this was aspirational at the time

There are three main types of documentation that we are concerned with in this book:

- User documentation, describing to the user how the system works and how to interact with it in order to achieve the desired results. There is a school of thought that this should be the first document written and should therefore form the specification. In a waterfall methodology this may work, but not in others. The structure of the user documentation should be derived from the Use Case[xii] (see chapter 13 of the companion volume for a closer look at Use Cases).
- Technical documentation, describing to technical staff how to maintain the code (including in-code documentation: see below), how to install it and what to do when something goes wrong. At UCLH we have a document called a "Panic File" for those occasions where, if it did not exist, that is what you would do. This technical file (which includes the technical design) is often required when seeking certification such as a CE mark. A technical file may be accessed in three possible circumstances and should be written with these in mind:
  - Routine maintenance
  - Emergency maintenance
  - Enhancement implementation
- Safety documentation (see safety cases on page 51).

[xii] A Use Case can help capture the requirements of a system in a simple diagram. It consists of actors (someone or something that uses the system), the system, Use Cases (things that may be done by the system) and relationships.

Chapter 8 – Databases: The use of spreadsheets, flat-file and structured databases

Whilst data can be stored in many ways and in many formats, in order to be useful the storage must contain structure. It has been noted earlier (page 6) that "Data + Structure = Information" and therefore we need structure to turn data into information.

The simplest data structure is the list: a single column of items. Arranging this list alphabetically (for example) brings further structure to the data and enables it to be used for rapid look-ups, using simple algorithms such as binary chop[i].

It is a simple step to expand this list structure into multiple columns, allowing the overall structure to then be sorted by any one of the columns in order to yield different information. A basic spreadsheet[ii] forms one such database. This information can equally be represented as a set of text with one line per row in the spreadsheet. This however introduces two new problems: how to separate the data in each row; and how to uniquely identify each row. Both of these are addressed by the spreadsheet structure, but not by the extracted data, or "flat file".

A flat file has no internal hierarchy, containing records that have no structured interrelationship. A typical flat file is a text file, containing no (or having had removed) word processing or other structure characters or markup (such as paragraph mark, tabs etc.). For example:

> Snail Brian Magic Roundabout brian@roundabout.com Flowerpot Bill Garden bill@weed.co.uk Cat Bagpuss Shop Window bagpuss@catworld.net Miller Windy The Windmill, Trumpton wmiller@chigley.ac.uk

A flat file can be given some structure by adding three things: a line separator; a unique identifier on each line; and a unique separator between each item in the lines[iii]. Taking the third solution first, the most common separator is the comma (hence "comma separated values", or CSV, a common file format used for data exchange[iv]) although this can produce problems of its own when recording data containing commas, for example addresses. There are two common solutions to this: encapsulating the data within double inverted commas; and using an "escape character" (see the next paragraph). The first of these brings problems where double inverted commas are also present (e.g. addresses). The second, although more robust, requires slightly more processing.

An "escape character" is a character that changes the interpretation of the one that follows it. A common escape character is "\". Hence, a comma that separates data would stand alone: , whereas a comma that should be taken to be part of the data would be preceded: \, . This notation does not suffer from the others mentioned above, as a backslash simply becomes \\.

Returning to the problem of adding structure to a flat file we examine the unique identifier. A unique identifier may not need to be added, of course, if a part of the data is already unique. Such an item (whether added or already present) is called the "primary key" and its importance will become clearer as more structure and abstraction are added to our data. A Spreadsheet already contains this identifier, in that each item of data can be uniquely referenced using its row and column identifiers.

---

[i] An algorithm where the ordered data is divided into two parts and the mid-point examined. If the sought data is before it, then the latter half can be ignored. If the sought data is after this mid-point, then the first half can be ignored. The search then repeats on the half of interest until the sought item is found.

[ii] i.e. one without any formulae or computed cells

[iii] There is some debate over this as many common flat file formats include line separators. Strictly, they shouldn't, but in practice they often do.

[iv] A CSV file is one in which table data is placed in lines of ASCII text with the value from each table cell separated by a comma and each row represented by a new line. A CSV file is one of the most common flat files, as it represents relational data in a text file

This leads us onto the relational model of data, first proposed by Codd in 1969 and subsequently revised. The concept was introduced in a paper "A Relational Model of Data for Large Shared Data Banks".[75] Modern relational databases simply implement a model that approximates the mathematical model defined by Codd. The relational model "*views information in a database as a collection of distinctly named tables. Each table has a specified set of named columns, each column name (also called an attribute) being distinct within a particular table, but not necessarily between tables. The entries within a particular column of a table must be atomic (that is, single data items) and all of the same type.*"[76]

Terminology

Relational database: A data structure through which data is stored in tables that are related to one another in some way. The way the tables are related is described through a relationship (see later definitions).

Data: values stored in a database.

Entity: A person, place, thing, or event about which we want to record information; an object we're interested in.

Field: The smallest structure in a relational database, used to store the individual pieces of data about the object; represents an attribute.

Record: A single "row" in a table; the collection of information for a single occurrence of the entity that the table represents.

Table: The chief structure in a relational database, composed of fields and records, whose physical order is unimportant[v]. A single table collects together all of the information we are tracking for a single entity and represents that entity.

Surname	Forename	Address	e-mail
Snail	Brian	Magic Roundabout	brian@roundabout.com
Flowerpot	Bill	Garden	bill@weed.co.uk
Cat	Bagpuss	Shop Window	bagpuss@catworld.net
Miller	Windy	The Windmill, Trumpton	wmiller@chigley.ac.uk

Figure 54:A Set of Data Arranged in a Table

The items in the first row are field names (but may also be thought of as column headings)

---

[v] As the order is placed on the table externally

Surname	Forename	Address	e-mail
Snail	Brian	Magic Roundabout	brian@roundabout.com
Flowerpot	Bill	Garden	bill@weed.co.uk
Cat	Bagpuss	Shop Window	bagpuss@catworld.net
Miller	Windy	The Windmill, Trumpton	wmiller@chigley.ac.uk

Table

Figure 55: The Table Labelled to Show the Terminology Described Above

An entity in this case is equivalent to a record

The goals of database design

The goals are to:

- understand your data and why you're tracking it
- eliminate duplication of data
- eliminate redundant data
- eliminate meaningless data or data that is irrelevant
- promote accuracy of data
- promote consistency of data
- make sure we can retrieve the information we need from the database
- support the business functions that use the database
- build a database that lends itself to future growth

Example

Let us now examine a specific example. Sam and Dakota decide to merge their music collections. Being computer scientists, they decide to create a database to catalogue the full collection. Their first attempt is a single-table database, such as described above:

Fields:

Media	CD/DVD/LP/MD/Tape/MP3 etc.
Artist	
Title	
Track1	
Track2	
(etc.)	
Price	In pence
Copies	
Total value	In pence

Sample row (with just 3 tracks for simplicity):

CD	Example	Playing in the Shadows	Skies Don't Lie	Stay Awake	Changed the Way You Kiss Me	999	2	1998

It is clear that this design is inefficient, and an inefficient design is difficult to maintain.

More terminology

> **Entity-Relationship Diagram (ERD):** Identifies the data/information required by displaying the relevant entities and the relationships between them. In a database project, the ERD is the database schema.
>
> **Key**: a field in the database (or an attribute in an ERD) that is used to uniquely identify records and establish relationships between tables or entities; used for the retrieval of data in the table.
>
> **Primary Key**: uniquely identifies each record in a table, the primary key is part of the table for which it operates. (Note that this is normally a single field but may be a combination of fields – a **composite key**).
>
> **Foreign Key**: A key from another table that is used to define a relationship to another record in another table. It has the same name and properties as the primary key from which it is copied.
>
> Rules for foreign keys:
>
>> 1-1: The primary key from the main table is inserted into the second table
>>
>> 1-Many: The primary key from the "1" table gets inserted into the "many" table
>>
>> Many-many: The primary key from each side gets placed into a third intermediate linking table that (usually) includes nothing but both keys.
>
> **Non-key**: a "regular" field; describes a characteristic of the table's subject.
>
> **Relationship**: Establishes a connection or correspondence or link between a pair of tables in a database, or between a pair of entities in an ERD.
>
> **One-to-one relationship**[vi]: A single record in table A is related to only one record in table B, and vice versa.
>
> **One-to-many relationship**: A single record in table A can be related to one or more records in table B, but a single record in table B can be related to only one record in table A. One-to-many may be one-to-many (mandatory) where each record in the one table must have at least one entry in the many table; and one-to-many (optional) where zero related records in the many table are allowed (e.g. patient, clinic and admission tables where the patient is only recorded when they have a clinic appointment so has records in that table, but may not have been admitted and so may not have any in that one).
>
> **Many-to-many relationship**: A single record in table A can be related to one or more records in table B, and vice versa. There are problems with many-to-many relationships in that one of the tables will contain a large amount of redundant data; both tables will contain some duplicate data; it will be difficult to add/update/delete records because of the duplication of fields between tables.
>
> **Notation:** There are many notations used to describe one-to-many relationships in an ERD. In the diagram on page 89 a simple "1" or "M" at opposite ends of the line indicating a relationship is used. Others include:

[vi] This and the following two relationships are intentionally similar to the rules for foreign keys.

UML:

Crow's foot (used in MySQL Workbench):

Barker (used in Oracle):

MS Access:

Example – making the design more efficient

First we eliminate columns from the same table, creating a new column to hold this data.

Change Track1, Track2 etc. into Tracks.

Media	Artist	Title	Tracks	Price	Copies	Value
CD	Example	Playing in the Shadows	Skies Don't Lie	999	2	1998
CD	Example	Playing in the Shadows	Stay Awake	999	2	1998
CD	Example	Playing in the Shadows	Changed the Way You Kiss Me	999	2	1998

We then create separate tables for each group of related data (there is only one in this example) and identify each row with a unique column (the primary key – called "Item_ID" here).

Item_ID	Media	Artist	Title	Tracks	Track_No	Price	Copies	Value
1	CD	Example	Playing in the Shadows	Skies Don't Lie	1	999	2	1998
2	CD	Example	Playing in the Shadows	Stay Awake	2	999	2	1998
3	CD	Example	Playing in the Shadows	Changed the Way You Kiss Me	3	999	2	1998

This is known as **first normal form** or **1NF**. Note that field names do not contain spaces or punctuation. Whilst some systems allow this, delimiters are then required.

To move to **second normal form** or **2NF**, we must remove subsets of data that apply to multiple rows of a table and place them in separate rows and create relationships between these new tables and their predecessors through the use of foreign keys. Here, the subsets are the Artist, the Title and the Track[vii]. These new tables also require primary

---

[vii] It could be argued that the Track is not a subset – however, a compilation album by the same artist will contain the same track name as the original album. Likewise, an album owned on multiple formats will contain the same tracks.

keys, called Artist_ID, Title_ID and Track_ID respectively. These primary keys are then stored in the original table as foreign keys, creating the relationship between the tables.

i.e.

Item_ID	Media	Artist_ID	Title_ID	Track_ID	Track_No	Price	Copies	Value
1	CD	1	1	1	1	999	2	1998
2	CD	1	1	2	2	999	2	1998
3	CD	1	1	3	3	999	2	1998

Artist_ID	Artist
1	Example

Title_ID	Title
1	Playing in the Shadows

Track_ID	Track
1	Skies Don't Lie
2	Stay Awake
3	Changed the Way You Kiss Me

Finally, to move to third normal form or 3NF, we must remove columns that are not fully dependent upon the primary key. In this example, the fields Media, Price and Copies move to the Title table (where they are dependent on the Primary Key) and the field Value is removed, as it can be computed from the fields Price and Copies.

i.e.

Item_ID	Artist_ID	Title_ID	Track_ID	Track_No
1	1	1	1	1
2	1	1	2	2
3	1	1	3	3

Artist_ID	Artist
1	Example

Title_ID	Title	Media	Price	Copies
1	Playing in the Shadows	CD	999	2

Track_ID	Track
1	Skies Don't Lie
2	Stay Awake
3	Changed the Way You Kiss Me

We can see that this final structure has the following relationships (naming the tables Item, Artist, Title and Track respectively):

- Artist to Item is one-to-many.
- Title to Item is one-to-many.
- Track to Item is one-to-one.

In this simple example there is little efficiency gained from this abstraction, but by the addition of just one extra field (track length) it can be seen how this structure is more adaptable than the one we started with.

The table Item has a primary key (Item_ID) and many foreign keys (Artist_ID etc.) which are the primary keys in their own tables. An analogy from programming would be the use of pointers: not the data itself, but a link to where the data may be found (an analogy with the World Wide Web is similar).

A structure like this is dependent on and representative of the relationships between the data and is known as a **Relational Database**. 4NF and 5NF also exist but are beyond the scope of this book.

The three normal forms may be summed up as follows:

- Duplicate columns within the same table are eliminated. (1NF)
- Each group of related data is in its own table with a primary key to identify each row. (1NF)
- Subsets applying to multiple rows of a table are in their own table. (2NF)
- Relationships are maintained by creating foreign keys. (2NF)
- Any columns not dependent upon the primary key are removed from the table. (3NF)

An amendment to third normal form was proposed by Codd and Boyce in 1974 to address certain possible anomalies that may arise in 3NF. BCNF (Boyce-Codd Normal Form, sometimes rendered 3.5NF) is thus a slight variant on 3NF, and the terms are often used interchangeably as most data structures will not fall foul of the subtlety[viii].

One issue does arise through the use of normalising a database, however. The relationships are achieved through the use of indexes. These are rapidly-changing files which therefore have a risk of corruption. If a corrupt index is used to retrieve records matching a certain key, then the records returned may not all match that key. It is therefore imperative (depending on the criticality of the data retrieved) that this data is checked prior to use. This can be as simple as ensuring that each returned record does contain the key searched for. This will ensure that no erroneous results are used, but does not ensure that all results have been returned. To achieve this, a redundant data item,

---

[viii] See https://en.wikipedia.org/wiki/Boyce%E2%80%93Codd_normal_form for an example of a database that does.

such as a child record counter[ix], must be used. In most cases, this is not an issue but it does need to be considered when the criticality of the results is high (e.g. a pharmacy system).

Structured Query Language (SQL)

Operations on relational databases are often carried out using **Structured Query Language** (SQL). As with any language there are various dialects, but the underlying principles are the same. The four most common commands are SELECT, INSERT, UPDATE and DELETE. Commands do not need to be in upper case, but are written this way here for clarity. The basic structure of a SELECT command is:

> SELECT {fields} FROM {table} WHERE {condition}

e.g. in the example above, "SELECT Track FROM Track WHERE Track_ID = 2" will return one result: "Stay Awake". The WHERE clause is a logical statement (using Boolean logic and can therefore include Boolean operators) which will evaluate to either TRUE or FALSE. The statement thus finds all rows for which the WHERE clause is TRUE and then returns the fields listed in the SELECT clause.

In order to make use of the relational structure, however, we need to return data from more than one table. There are two main ways of doing this:

> SELECT {fields} FROM {tables} WHERE {condition, including the relationship}

And

> SELECT {fields} FROM {table} JOIN {table} ON {relationship} WHERE {condition}

Examples of these might be:

> SELECT Artist.Artist[x], Track.Track FROM Artist, Track, Item WHERE Artist.Artist_ID = Item.Artist_ID AND Track.Track_ID = Item.Track_ID AND Item.Title_ID=1

Which returns

Artist	Track
Example	Skies Don't Lie
Example	Stay Awake
Example	Changed the Way You Kiss Me

The notation "Table.Field" can become unwieldy and so an alias[xi] can be used to make the statement easier to read:

> SELECT a.Artist, t.Track FROM Artist a, Track t, Item i WHERE a.Artist_ID = i.Artist_ID AND t.Track_ID = i.Track_ID and i.Title_ID=1

The notation "Artist a" (in the FROM clause) provides an alias for the table name which can be used throughout the command.

The second form, in order to achieve the same result, might be written as:

[ix] A field that stores the number of records linked to this one

[x] The syntax is Table.Field and is used so that each field is uniquely identified. The importance of this can be seen from the table structures: several field names appear in multiple tables (as can be seen from the WHERE clause) – SQL requires that no ambiguity exists in the statement.

[xi] An abbreviation

SELECT a.Artist, t.Track FROM Item i JOIN Artist a ON a.Artist_ID = i.Artist_ID JOIN Track t ON t.Track_ID = i.Track_ID WHERE i.Title_ID=1

A wildcard (*) will list all fields, e.g.

SELECT * FROM Artist

Will list all artist names and ID numbers in the database.

An INSERT statement adds a record to a single table. To add the track "The Way" to the example above would require the following statements:

INSERT INTO Item (Item_ID, Artist_ID, Title_ID, Track_ID, Track_No) VALUES (4, 1, 1, 4, 3)

INSERT INTO Track (Track_ID, Track) VALUES (4, "The Way")

This gives the resultant tables:

Table **Item**

Item_ID	Artist_ID	Title_ID	Track_ID	Track_No
1	1	1	1	1
2	1	1	2	2
3	1	1	3	3
4	1	1	4	3[xii]

Table **Track**

Track_ID	Track
1	Skies Don't Lie
2	Stay Awake
3	Changed the Way You Kiss Me
4	The Way

The field list is not always necessary: if the list is omitted it is assumed that the values are in the same order as the fields. If the primary key is an Autonumber field (i.e. one that the system increments and assigns) then this cannot be specified, meaning that the field list is required. (If the primary key is an Autonumber field, then adding data may require several steps, for the value assigned will have to be retrieved so it can be provided to the other INSERT statements).

An UPDATE statement has the form:

UPDATE {table} SET {field1=value1, field2=value2, …} WHERE {condition}

[xii] The error is intentional and will be corrected later

Two examples of statements to correct the error introduced by the INSERT example which has produced 2 track number 3s might be:

UPDATE Item SET Track_No=Track_no+1 WHERE Title_ID=1 AND Track_ID>3

UPDATE Item SET Track_No=4 WHERE Item_ID=4

Note that the first form may update multiple records, whereas the second will update only one as it uses the primary key to uniquely identify a single record.

Both forms give the same resultant table:

Table **Item**

Item_ID	Artist_ID	Title_ID	Track_ID	Track_No
1	1	1	1	1
2	1	1	2	2
3	1	1	3	3
4	1	1	4	4

Finally the DELETE statement has the form:

DELETE FROM {table} WHERE {condition}

If the condition is omitted, then all records from the specified table will be deleted. An example might be:

DELETE FROM Track WHERE Track_ID=4

This statement alone would create a referential integrity error, in that Item now refers to a record in Track that no longer exists. In order to correct this, either a new Track with Track_ID of 4 must be created, or the following must be done:

DELETE FROM Item WHERE Track_ID=4

This gives the resultant tables:

Table **Item**

Item_ID	Artist_ID	Title_ID	Track_ID	Track_No
1	1	1	1	1
2	1	1	2	2
3	1	1	3	3

Table **Track**

Track_ID	Track
1	Skies Don't Lie
2	Stay Awake
3	Changed the Way You Kiss Me

Relational databases are very common in hospital informatics and clinical computing. Examples include oncology management systems, equipment management systems, the electronic patient record and cardiology patient monitoring systems.

Some useful commands/functions
MAX() and MIN() work as you might expect, e.g.

> SELECT MAX(Track_No) FROM Item

Will return the largest track number (in this example, 3). It can then be used as part of a more complex SELECT, e.g.

> SELECT Title_ID FROM Item WHERE (Track_No)=(SELECT MAX(Track_No) FROM Item)

Will return the IDs of the highest numbered tracks (in this example, 3).

COUNT() returns the number of records matching the WHERE clause, rather than the records themselves. E.g.

> SELECT COUNT(Title) from Title WHERE Artist_ID=1

Will return the number of titles for the artist with ID of 1 (in this example, 1).

DAY(), MONTH() and YEAR() will return the required part of a date.

Chapter 9 – Regulation: the use of a computer as a clinical device

The Medical Devices Directive (MDD)

The Medical Devices Directive of 1993 (less well-known as Directive 93/42/EEC) contained within it a definition of a medical device. This definition (below) lies at the heart of all subsequent directives, regulations and guidance.

The Directive defines a 'medical device' as meaning "*any instrument, apparatus, appliance, material or other article, whether used alone or in combination, including the software necessary for its proper application intended by the manufacturer to be used for human beings for the purpose of:*

> *- diagnosis, prevention, monitoring, treatment or alleviation of disease,*
>
> *- diagnosis, monitoring, treatment, alleviation of or compensation for an injury or handicap,*
>
> *- investigation, replacement or modification of the anatomy or of a physiological process,*
>
> *- control of conception,*

and which does not achieve its principal intended action in or on the human body by pharmacological, immunological or metabolic means, but which may be assisted in its function by such means." (This is part 1.2a of the Directive as mentioned in the following flowchart).

It is worth noting that accessories (defined as "*an article which whilst not being a device is intended specifically by its manufacturer to be used together with a device to enable it to be used in accordance with the use of the device intended by the manufacturer of the device*") are treated as Medical Devices in their own right and must be classified, examined and regulated as though they were independent.

There have been several additional Directives (2003, 2005 and 2007[i]) which have modified the original Directive. Generally these modifications have been to increase the scope of the Directive to cover more types of device. At the time of writing, the most recent technical revision is Directive 2007/47/EC. The interest in this directive from the point of view of this course lies in items 6 and 20 and article 1. Article 1 re-defines a medical device adding the word "software" to the list, becoming "*any instrument, apparatus, appliance, software, material or other article*". The effect of this is to mean that software alone may be defined as a medical device and not just when it is incorporated within hardware defined as a medical device. This is made clear by item 6 of this revision, which states:

"*It is necessary to clarify that software in its own right, when specifically intended by the manufacturer to be used for one or more of the medical purposes set out in the definition of a medical device, is a medical device. Software for general purposes when used in a healthcare setting is not a medical device.*"

The ability to run software that is a medical device on a computer that is not originally designed as a medical device thus re-designates the hardware as a medical device and must be evaluated and controlled accordingly. The non-mandatory guidance document "Qualification and Classification of stand alone software" provides decision flowcharts and definitions in order to assist the determination as to whether stand-alone software is a medical device and, if so, the class to which it belongs. Without repeating the full content here, it is worth noting that it is recognised that software may consist of multiple modules, some of which are medical devices and some of which are not[ii].

Item 20 of the revision states: "*Taking account of the growing importance of software in the field of medical devices, be it as stand alone or as software incorporated in a device, validation of software in accordance with the state of the art should be an essential requirement.*" And is covered in chapter 7 on testing.

---

[i] Although the year of adoption is not the same as the year of implementation
[ii] Indeed, an individual algorithm may be a medical device.

A medical device may be classified as Class I (including Is & Im), Class IIa, IIb and III, with Class III covering the highest risk products[iii].

Classification of a medical device will depend upon a series of factors, including:

- *"how long the device is intended to be in continuous use*

- *whether or not the device is invasive or surgically invasive,*

- *whether the device is implantable or active*

- *whether or not the device contains a substance, which in its own right is considered to be a medicinal substance and has action ancillary to that of the device."*[77]

The classification rules are set out in Annex IX of the directive which includes definitions of the terminology used in the classification rules[iv].

[iii] Put simply, Class I is low risk, IIa low-to-medium, IIb medium-to-high and III high risk.
[iv] There are some flowcharts to assist with classification on the cited web site.

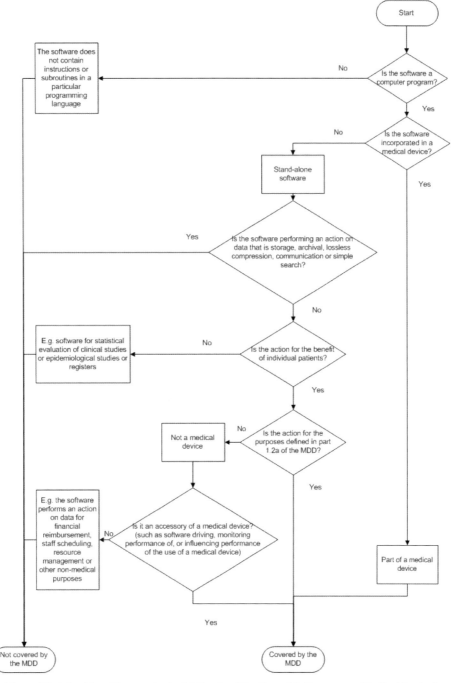

Figure 56: A Decision Diagram to Assist the Qualification of Software as a Medical Device[v]

The Medical Devices Regulations (MDR)

One of the cornerstones of the EU is the free movement of goods. This means that a product that is allowed on the market in one of the Member States is also allowed on the markets of other Member States. This concept is enabled

---

[v] Further explanations are available at
https://assets.publishing.service.gov.uk/government/uploads/system/uploads/attachment_data/file/717865/Software_flow_chart_Ed_1-05.pdf

by three conditions within the 2016 version of the "Blue Guide" on the implementation of EU products, which must be met:

1. Essential requirements for the products involved must be defined;
2. Methods must be established to describe how product compliance with the requirements is addressed;
3. Mechanisms to supervise and control the actions of all Economic Operators and others involved in the manufacturing and distribution of the products must be created.

The predecessors of the **Medical Devices Regulation** (MDR) – the **Active Implantable Medical Devices Directive** (AIMDD) 90/385/EEC and the **Medical Devices Directive** (MDD) 93/42/EEC – achieved this. They defined Essential Requirements, introduced harmonised standards helping to demonstrate conformity to the Essential Requirements, defined conformity assessment procedures, and organised market surveillance functions by **Competent Authorities** (CAs) and **Notified Bodies** (NBs).

The Directives had some inherent weaknesses, though. Changes in technology and medical science demanded additional legislation and the interpretation of the Directives was not consistent across all national governments. Directive 2007/47/EC modified the MDD and AIMDD in an attempt to address these concerns, but this amendment did not achieve all goals. The scandal involving defective breast implants manufactured by Poly Implant Prosthesis (PIP) in France demonstrated additional weaknesses in the system.

The major difference between a regulation and a directive is that a directive has to be taken and put into member state law through each different legislative system (thus giving scope for different interpretations in different member states), whereas a regulation becomes law as written in all member states. There is no room for differences of interpretation or application unless explicitly stated in the regulation that aspects are left up to member states.

The MDR came into force in 2017. Member states had until 2020 in which to implement it, meaning that most requirements will not fully apply until 26th May 2020 for Medical Devices, and 26th May 2022 for In Vitro Diagnostic Medical Devices[vi]. It *"lays down rules concerning the placing on the market, making available on the market or putting into service of medical devices for human use and accessories for such devices in the Union. This Regulation also applies to clinical investigations concerning such medical devices and accessories conducted in the Union."*[78]

The MDR has 175[vii] pages and is vastly more "legal" than the MDD, which took more of a good will approach. It will thus result in far more work for the regulators.

The MDD focussed on the path to CE marking, whereas the MDR promotes a life-cycle approach (in this it is similar to the US' **Food and Drug Administration** (FDA) and many other international standards).

Previous guidance documents (MEDDEVs) have been incorporated into the regulation[viii]. This has made the optional guidance mandatory. Clinical data and evaluations will have greater emphasis and equivalence[ix] will be more rigorously interpreted, increasing the challenge for demonstrating performance of clinical safety for medical devices.

[vi] The Implementation date for Medical Devices was postponed to May 26, 2021, due to COVID-19.

[vii] Although the first 15 pages are known as Recitals; so Recital (19) is relevant to software and Recital (30) is relevant to in-house manufacture. They 'set the scene' but are not requirements. In Standards speak, they are 'informative' and not 'normative'.

[viii] Possibly not all, but certainly Guidance on Authorized Representation, Clinical Evaluation, Vigilance, and Post-Market Clinical Follow-Up.

[ix] Previously references to studies done with other devices

Article 1 of the MDR[x] brings products without an intended medical purpose that are listed in Annex XVI into the scope of the MDR[xi]. Medical devices, accessories and the products in Annex XVI are referred to as "devices". In the definition of accessories, no exception is made for products without a medical purpose that will be considered medical devices and therefore their accessories will also fall within the scope of the MDR.

Annex XVI may have new groups of products added during the lifetime of the MDR.

Article 2 lists 71 definitions, compared to the MDD's 14. Amongst these, **In Vitro Diagnostics** (IVD) are covered and accessories are now defined to "assist" as well as "enable" a medical device's usage. Likewise, "label" is defined[xii], as is "risk"[xiii].

"Standalone software" is no longer mentioned. *"Software may have a medical purpose, in which case it falls within the scope of the MDR. Annex VIII, Classification Rules now refers to "software that drives a device or influences the use of a device" versus software that is "independent of any other device.""*[79]

The major definitions[xiv] (from a computing viewpoint) are:

"(1) 'medical device' means any instrument, apparatus, appliance, software, implant, reagent, material or other article intended by the manufacturer to be used, alone or in combination, for human beings for one or more of the following specific medical purposes:

— diagnosis, prevention, monitoring, prediction, prognosis[xv], treatment or alleviation of disease,

— diagnosis, monitoring, treatment, alleviation of, or compensation for, an injury or disability,

— investigation, replacement or modification of the anatomy or of a physiological or pathological process or state,

— providing information by means of in vitro examination of specimens derived from the human body, including organ, blood and tissue donations,

and which does not achieve its principal intended action by pharmacological, immunological or metabolic means, in or on the human body, but which may be assisted in its function by such means.

The following products shall also be deemed to be medical devices:

— devices for the control or support of conception;

— products specifically intended for the cleaning, disinfection or sterilisation of devices as referred to in Article 1(4) and of those referred to in the first paragraph of this point.

(2) 'accessory for a medical device' means an article which, whilst not being itself a medical device, is intended by its manufacturer to be used together with one or several particular medical device(s) to specifically enable the medical device(s) to be used in accordance with its/their intended purpose(s) or to specifically and directly assist the medical functionality of the medical device(s) in terms of its/their intended purpose(s);

---

[x] Articles are definitions – Annexes describe application

[xi] Such as contact lenses, substances or items created for facial or dermatological use by means of injection or another type of introduction (excluding tattoos) and high intensity electromagnetic radiation equipment for use on the body, as used in depilation and tattoo removal treatments. The Regulation considers that these types of products with an aesthetic rather than a medical purpose may be similar to medical devices in terms of functionality and risk profile, and as such must be considered medical devices.

[xii] The physical label on the device or package

[xiii] As per ISO EN 14971:2012 – Risk classification is in Annex 8.

[xiv] There is now only one definition of a medical device whereas previously there were three.

[xv] Prediction and prognosis are significant additions from the MDD's definition

(3) 'custom-made device' means any device specifically made in accordance with a written prescription of any person authorised by national law by virtue of that person's professional qualifications which gives, under that person's responsibility, specific design characteristics, and is intended for the sole use of a particular patient exclusively to meet their individual conditions and needs.

However, mass-produced devices which need to be adapted to meet the specific requirements of any professional user and devices which are mass-produced by means of industrial manufacturing processes in accordance with the written prescriptions of any authorised person shall not be considered to be custom-made devices;

(4) 'active device' means any device, the operation of which depends on a source of energy other than that generated by the human body for that purpose, or by gravity, and which acts by changing the density of or converting that energy. Devices intended to transmit energy, substances or other elements between an active device and the patient, without any significant change, shall not be deemed to be active devices.

Software shall also be deemed to be an active device[xvi];

…

(12) 'intended purpose' means the use for which a device is intended according to the data supplied by the manufacturer on the label, in the instructions for use or in promotional or sales materials or statements and as specified by the manufacturer in the clinical evaluation;

…

(25) 'compatibility' is the ability of a device, including software, when used together with one or more other devices in accordance with its intended purpose, to:

(a) perform without losing or compromising the ability to perform as intended, and/or

(b) integrate and/or operate without the need for modification or adaption of any part of the combined devices, and/or

(c) be used together without conflict/interference or adverse reaction.

(26) 'interoperability' is the ability of two or more devices, including software, from the same manufacturer or from different manufacturers, to:

(a) exchange information and use the information that has been exchanged for the correct execution of a specified function without changing the content of the data, and/or

(b) communicate with each other, and/or

(c) work together as intended.

(29) 'putting into service' means the stage at which a device, other than an investigational device, has been made available to the final user as being ready for use on the Union market for the first time for its intended purpose;

(30) 'manufacturer' means a natural or legal person who manufactures or fully refurbishes a device or has a device designed, manufactured or fully refurbished, and markets that device under its name or trademark;

(31) 'fully refurbishing', for the purposes of the definition of manufacturer, means the complete rebuilding of a device already placed on the market or put into service, or the making of a new device from used devices, to bring it into conformity with this Regulation, combined with the assignment of a new lifetime to the refurbished device;" [80]

[xvi] Previously passive – this may thus increase the risk rating of existing software.

Additionally, clause 19 from the preamble is worth mentioning[xvii]: "*It is necessary to clarify that software in its own right, when specifically intended by the manufacturer to be used for one or more of the medical purposes set out in the definition of a medical device, qualifies as a medical device, while software for general purposes, even when used in a healthcare setting, or software intended for life-style and well-being purposes is not a medical device. The qualification of software, either as a device or an accessory, is independent of the software's location or the type of interconnection between the software and a device.*" [81]

Chapter II – "Making Available On The Market And Putting Into Service Of Devices, Obligations Of Economic Operators, Reprocessing, CE Marking, Free Movement" provides substantive definitions and responsibilities but also delineates between the responsibilities of the **Authorized Representative** (AR), the distributor and the importer. Interestingly, "Distance sales" are regulated, meaning that devices sold to EU citizens through the Internet have to comply with the MDR[xviii]. Thus manufacturers of such devices must appoint ARs if they are not based in Europe.

Paragraph 4 of this chapter states: "*Devices that are manufactured and used within health institutions shall be considered as having been put into service.*" [82] but is tempered by Paragraph 5:

"*With the exception of the relevant general safety and performance requirements set out in Annex I, the requirements of this Regulation shall not apply to devices, manufactured and used only within health institutions established in the Union, provided that all of the following conditions are met:*

(a) the devices are not transferred to another legal entity[xix],

(b) manufacture and use of the devices occur under appropriate[xx] quality management systems,

(c) the health institution justifies in its documentation that the target patient group's specific needs cannot be met, or cannot be met at the appropriate level of performance by an equivalent[xxi] device available on the market,

(d) the health institution provides information upon request on the use of such devices to its competent authority, which shall include a justification of their manufacturing, modification and use;

(e) the health institution draws up a declaration which it shall make publicly available, including:

    (i) the name and address of the manufacturing health institution;

    (ii) the details necessary to identify the devices;

    (iii) a declaration that the devices meet the general safety and performance requirements set out in Annex I to this Regulation and, where applicable, information on which requirements are not fully met with a reasoned justification therefor,[xxii]

(f) the health institution draws up documentation that makes it possible to have an understanding of the manufacturing facility, the manufacturing process, the design and performance data of the devices, including the intended purpose, and that is sufficiently detailed to enable the competent authority to ascertain that the general safety and performance requirements set out in Annex I to this Regulation are met;

(g) the health institution takes all necessary measures to ensure that all devices are manufactured in accordance with the documentation referred to in point (f), and

---

[xvii] As it means that "Lifestyle" software (activity trackers etc.) are not classified as medical devices
[xviii] It is unclear how this will be controlled
[xix] Not defined, but clarification has been issued that the NHS is not a legal entity so responsibility falls to individual Trusts.
[xx] There is no definition as to what might be appropriate.
[xxi] What constitutes "equivalent" is ambiguous as it is based on the patient need, which is not very well defined. Effectively this clause insists that a device be CE marked if an equivalent CE-marked device already exists.
[xxii] A local website may be sufficient

(h) the health institution reviews experience gained from clinical use of the devices and takes all necessary corrective actions. Member States may require that such health institutions submit to the competent authority any further relevant information about such devices which have been manufactured and used on their territory.

Member States shall retain the right to restrict the manufacture and the use of any specific type of such devices and shall be permitted access to inspect the activities of the health institutions.

This paragraph shall not apply to devices that are manufactured on an industrial scale[xxiii]." [83]

"Article 10(8) of Chapter II requires the manufacturer to supply CAs with all information necessary to demonstrate conformity, as well as to share that information with patients or their representatives claiming compensation. These requirements will obviously have an impact on manufacturers' technical documentation." [84]

Article 10 also specifies requirements for custom-made devices, such that full technical documentation is not required but documentation in accordance with Section 2 of Annex XIII is. Custom-made and investigational devices are also exempt from the requirement to draw up an EU declaration of conformity. Investigational (but not custom-made) devices are exempt from the requirement to maintain a **Quality Management System** (QMS)[xxiv]. Article 5.5 (above) sets out the conditions for what the MHRA refer to as the **Health Institution Exemption** (HIE). If this light-touch regulation is not met, then the regulation applies in full[xxv].

Chapter II introduces the person responsible[xxvi] for regulatory compliance within the manufacturer or AR (Article 15). This employee should be highly educated and experienced.

Annex 1, the **General Safety and Performance Requirements** (GSPR) explains the "reduction of risk as far as possible" as reducing risk "without adversely affecting the risk benefit ratio." It also inserts the statement "*taking into account the generally acknowledged state of the art*" which will assist non-medical products treated as medical devices and products for which there are no sufficient standards.

The new GSPR checklist has more than 220 items to review[85] and includes the requirement for the manufacturer to use a risk management system.

Chapter 2, "requirements regarding design and manufacture", has added several sections, of which the most pertinent relating to software are:

- Software in devices and software that are devices in and of themselves;
- Risks concerning medical devices for lay persons.
- Possible negative interactions between medical device software and other IT are to be considered (see 80001-1:2021), as are the environments in which mobile computing platforms are used (sections 14, 14.2, 14.5, 15.1 and 17.3).

Chapter 3 contains the requirement for the label to state that the product is a medical device, leading to speculation[86] that this may lead to the introduction of a "MD" symbol equivalent to the current "IVD" one.

There are, as has been noted in the footnotes, some ambiguities and areas requiring clarification. One such is whether a new version of software is a new device, as is how software relates to the definitions on parts and components. Overall, though, the concepts and requirements of the MDR are recognised best practice enshrined in regulation.

[xxiii] Not defined

[xxiv] Meaning, of course, that all other in house manufacture devices must be controlled, usually by a QMS

[xxv] For an excellent discussion of this see "MDR – the Health Institution Exemption and MHRA draft guidance" by Justin McCarthy in Scope 27:3

[xxvi] "*at least one*" [xxvi] although small enterprises need not have such an employee but must "*have such person permanently and continuously at their disposal.*" [xxvi]

Scripts

There has been some confusion and debate regarding the subject of scripts (i.e. pieces of code that run on a medical device). One view is that they are covered by the device's CE mark as the device is intended to host scripts and therefore is operating as intended. This does not make the manufacturer liable for any errors in programming, however, as the author is still responsible for the safe application of the device (and therefore the script). Certainly, scripts that are actually recorded macros (designed to be re-played, even if edited slightly) are not MDs in their own right, they are simply the normal operation of the MD in question.

The alternative view is that scripts form software modules and therefore are independent. The MDD defined software as being able to be broken down into modules where each one correlates with an application of the software, some having a medical purpose and some not[87]. While the first view is probably the most accurate (certainly in the majority of cases where scripts mainly aggregate data), a risk analysis may reveal a requirement to treat the script as independent, thus leading to the second view.

Brexit

There is confusion as to how much (if at all) of the MDR will pass into UK law. At the time of writing, Great Britain will follow MDD based regulations until 2023[xxvii] and Northern Ireland will implement the MDR from May 2021. The UK MDR2002 was updated in Jan 2021[xxviii]. One of the main changes was the introduction of the **UKCA**[xxix] mark, which must be placed on medical devices placed on the GB market (note there are different rules for Northern Ireland, which has a **UKNI** mark). *"A UKCA mark is a logo that is placed on medical devices to show they conform to the requirements in the UK MDR 2002. It shows that the device is fit for its intended purpose stated and meets legislation relating to safety."*[88] It is worth noting that an explanatory memorandum to the UK MDR2002 says *"Any devices that are in conformity with EU legislation (MDD, AIMDD, IVDD, MDR, IVDR) can continue to be placed on the market in GB until 30 June 2023. This is to provide manufacturers with time to adjust to future GB regulations that will be consulted on and published at a later date."*[89] This has given businesses longer to apply UKCA marking (originally January 2022 – although current guidance says they must be ready to apply it by January 2023[90]).

On 1/8/23 the UK Government announced that the implementation of the UKCA had been delayed "indefinitely". *"The move has delighted business groups, which had been lobbying hard against the prospect of firms that sell into the much larger EU market having to carry out two separate sets of safety tests, with two separate regulatory bodies"*[91].

There is great similarity between the UK MDR2002 and the MDD – the MHRA's advice contains flowcharts on conformity with the instruction to read "CE marking" as "UKCA marking" and any reference to Competent Authority as "MHRA".

The UK MDR 2002 encapsulates these directives:

- Directive 90/385/EEC on active implantable medical devices (EU AIMDD)

- Directive 93/42/EEC on medical devices (EU MDD)

- Directive 98/79/EC on in vitro diagnostic medical devices (EU IVDD)

This means that since 1 January 2021, the Great Britain route to market and UKCA marking requirements are still based on the requirements derived from current EU legislation.

Regardless, the following will be true:

[xxvii] Updated to 2025 in 2023
[xxviii] The latest guidance is at https://www.gov.uk/guidance/regulating-medical-devices-in-the-uk
[xxix] UK Conformity Assessed

All medical devices, active implantable medical devices, IVDs and custom-made devices will need to be registered with the MHRA prior to being placed on the UK market. As this is an extension to the existing registration requirements, there will be a grace period to allow time for compliance with the new registration process:

- 4 months: Class III medical devices, Class IIb implantable medical devices, Active implantable medical devices, IVD List A
- 8 months: Class IIb non-implantable medical devices, Class IIa medical devices, IVD List B, Self-test IVDs
- 12 months: Class I medical devices, Self-certified IVDs, Class A IVDs

The MDR regulations will still be adopted within the UK[xxx]. However, the UK will be treated as being a "3rd country" – that is, a country outside of the EU27. For European medical devices imported to the UK, UK based importers & distributors will no longer be treated as European distributors (i.e. almost as if they were within the same country as the manufacturer). Instead, European medical device manufacturers will need an AR established within the UK to:

- ensure & maintain conformity
- communicate with the Secretary of State upon request
- provide PMS (Post Market Surveillance)
- inform the manufacturers about complaints & reports
- terminate the legal relationship with the manufacturer in the event the manufacturer acts contrary to its obligations.

The Cumberledge report[xxxi] recommended that UK legislation be at least as stringent as the EU MDR, so the pragmatic advice would seem to be to follow the EU MDR.

The UK has introduced a new **Medical Device Information System** (MDIS) with which all MDs manufactured in the UK (or have a UK Responsible Person) have to be registered. Initially only Class 1, custom-made and IVD devices were required to be registered but all others were to be done by September 2021. The MDIS is accessible to the public, although hospitals and suppliers are more likely to use it.

The Government's response to the 2021 consultation gave reason to believe that there will be a formal 'in-house exemption' from full conformity assessment and UKCA marking for devices made and used within the same health institution, provided certain conditions are met, and these conditions are broadly in-line with those in the EU MDR – meeting relevant essential requirements, developing and manufacturing in-house devices under a QMS, documentation retention, adverse incident reporting etc. The response indicates that there will be a requirement to register in-house devices with MHRA and to register clinical investigations and performance studies. There is a further hint towards the possibility of a more open approach to providing in-house devices from one HI to another, provided this is not for commercial or profitable purposes.

Artificial Intelligence (AI)

The NHS has recognised the importance of regulating AI use in healthcare to ensure that patient safety and privacy are protected. In April 2021, the NHS introduced a new regulatory framework for AI in healthcare called the NHS AI Lab[92]. This is designed to support the ethical development and safe deployment of AI technologies in healthcare. Additionally, the UK government also established the Centre for Data Ethics and Innovation (CDEI), an independent advisory body that provides guidance and advice on the ethical use of data and AI technologies.

Another initiative to ensure the safety, efficacy, and reliability of machine learning-based medical devices is the Good Machine Learning Practice (GMLP)[93]. It is a set of 10 guiding principles jointly identified by the U.S. Food and Drug Administration (FDA), Health Canada and the UK MHRA. The principles and practices are intended to promote safe, effective and high-quality medical devices that use AI and ML whilst ensuring that the development, testing,

---

[xxx] Imported devices will have been manufactured to them and exporters will need to comply with them.
[xxxi] The **Independent Medicines and Medical Devices Safety** (IMMDS) Review was commissioned in February 2018 and the report, "First do no harm" was published in July 2020.

and deployment of machine learning-based medical devices are done in accordance with recognised quality standards, and that they are consistent with regulatory requirements.

National Regulators: FDA and MHRA

The **Food and Drug Administration** (FDA, USA) and **Medicines and Healthcare products Regulatory Authority** (MHRA, UK) are national regulators setting standards of compliance which must be achieved before a product can be placed on the market in the relevant country. Additionally, the MHRA is the CA for medical devices and medicines regulation in the UK.

FDA regulations are generally regarded as being "tougher" than MHRA ones, although whether this refers to the stringency of the regulations or the regulation process is unclear. The main difference is that MHRA is concerned with safety, whilst the FDA is also concerned about clinical effectiveness. In the UK that is a separate role, dealt with by **The National Institute for Health and Clinical Excellence** (NICE). The FDA *"is responsible for protecting the public health by ensuring the safety, efficacy, and security of human and veterinary drugs, biological products, and medical devices; and by ensuring the safety of our nation's food supply, cosmetics, and products that emit radiation"* and *"for regulating the manufacturing, marketing, and distribution of tobacco products to protect the public health and to reduce tobacco use by minors"* as well as *"advancing the public health by helping to speed innovations that make medical products more effective, safer, and more affordable and by helping the public get the accurate, science-based information they need to use medical products and foods to maintain and improve their health."*[94] It is the medical device remit that is of interest here.

Devices are regulated under the **Federal Food, Drug and Cosmetics** Act (FD&C Act) as amended by the Medical Device Amendments 1976. As in the EU, the definition of a medical device is under review and the change of definition mainly concerns types of health-related software that will no longer be defined as medical devices and thus will no longer be regulated by the FDA. This includes most types of **Clinical Decision Support** (CDS) software, 'general wellness' apps (e.g. fit-bit type) and what the FDA calls **Medical Device Data System** (MDDS) software, i.e. software intended to *"transfer, store, convert formats, and display medical device data"*[95]. This will bring the US system more in line with the EU Regulations.

Premarket Approval (PMA)[xxxii] is the most stringent type of device marketing application required by the FDA[96] and is based on a determination by the FDA that the PMA contains sufficient valid scientific evidence providing reasonable assurance that the device is safe and effective for its intended use or uses. It is only required for Class III devices however. One interesting form of regulation the FDA offers is humanitarian device exemption. This is a form of PMA but is for **Humanitarian Use Devices** (HUD). These are devices that are intended to benefit patients by treating or diagnosing a disease or condition that affects not more than than 8,000 individuals in the United States per year. Thus the "effectiveness" section of a full PMA submission is not required.

The UK's regulator of medicines, medical devices and blood components for transfusion, responsible for ensuring their safety, quality and effectiveness, is the MHRA. It is worth emphasising that the "A" in MHRA is "Agency" and not "Authority" and as such they are an executive agency of the Department of Health. The agency is responsible for:

- *"ensuring that medicines, medical devices and blood components for transfusion meet applicable standards of safety, quality and efficacy*
- *ensuring that the supply chain for medicines, medical devices and blood components is safe and secure*
- *promoting international standardisation and harmonisation to assure the effectiveness and safety of biological medicines*
- *helping to educate the public and healthcare professionals about the risks and benefits of medicines, medical devices and blood components, leading to safer and more effective use*

---

xxxii As the name implies, PMA is required before a product can be placed on the market.

- *supporting innovation and research and development that's beneficial to public health*
- *influencing UK, EU and international regulatory frameworks so that they're risk-proportionate and effective at protecting public health"*[97]

Additionally, in 2021 the Medicines and Medical Devices Act established the role of the **Patient Safety Commissioner** (PSC) for England[xxxiii], in response to the Cumberledge Report. The Commissioner's core duties are to promote the safety of patients with regard to the use of medicines and medical devices, and to promote the importance of the views of patients and other members of the public in relation to the safety of medicines and medical devices.

Recalls
Additionally, both the FDA and MHRA issue alerts and recalls. It is therefore important that a healthcare provider has someone tasked with receiving these and disseminating the information appropriately, although only from their own agency (i.e. the NHS need not receive FDA alerts, but must act upon **Field Safety Notices** (FSN)).

From a Medical Physics/Clinical Engineering perspective, therefore, there are three main areas where interaction with MHRA/FDA is required:

- Ensuring that devices deployed have the correct accreditation/approval.
- Determining when in-house developments require accreditation/approval (and seeking it when it is required).
- Receiving and disseminating alerts and recalls.

CE marking
Directive 2007/47/EC embraces the concept of software as a medical device and therefore clearly links it to a discussion of CE[xxxiv] marking, which concludes this section. The key points are that CE marking on a product:

- is a manufacturer's declaration that the product complies with the essential requirements of the relevant European health, safety and environmental protection legislation.
- indicates to governmental officials that the product may be legally placed on the market in their country.
- ensures the free movement of the product within the **European Free Trade Association** (EFTA) & **European Union** (EU) single market (total 27 countries), and
- permits the withdrawal of the non-conforming products by customs and enforcement/vigilance authorities.

CE marking did not originally encompass Medical Devices, but they were brought into the scope of the general directive by a series of subsequent directives from 2000 onwards. It is worth noting that a device must comply with all relevant directives (i.e. all the ones that apply to it).

EU directives often use a series of questions in order to classify the level of risk and then refer to a chart called "Conformity Assessment Procedures". This chart includes all of the acceptable options available to a manufacturer to certify their product and affix the CE mark.

Products with minimal risk can be self-certified, where the manufacturer prepares a *"Declaration of Conformity"* and affixes the CE mark to their own product. Products with greater risk are usually (depending on the directive) independently certified, which must be done by a "*Notified Body*".

[xxxiii] Which presumably covers Wales. Scotland has established a PSC Specialist Reference Group.
[xxxiv] "CE" is an abbreviation of the French phrase "Conformité Européene" ("European Conformity"). Whilst the original term was "EC Mark", it was officially replaced by "CE Marking" in the Directive 93/68/EEC in 1993 which is now used in all EU official documents.

A Notified Body is an organisation that has been nominated by a member government and has been notified by the European Commission. They serve as independent test labs and perform the steps required by directives. Manufacturers are not required to use notified bodies in their own country, but may use any within the EU.

Custom made devices, devices undergoing clinical investigation and in-vitro medical devices for clinical investigation do not currently require CE marks but must be marked 'exclusively for clinical investigation'.

The MHRA is the UK body that provides advice and guidance on matters concerning the relationship between the MDD and the CE requirements and their website[98] contains helpful documents.

Other standards
Three international standards offer valuable contributions to those working to provide and support Medical Devices:

- IEC 62304-2015: Medical Device Software Lifecycle - Software Lifecycle processes. This offers a risk based approach and makes reference to the use of **Software of Unknown Provenance** (SOUP).
- IEC/ISO 90003-2004 Guidelines for the application of ISO 9000-2000 to computer software, which offers similar concepts to those embraced in the TickIT scheme[74].
- ISO 13485-2003 Medical Devices - Quality Management Systems - Requirements for Regulatory Purposes. This deals with the production and management of Medical Devices in a manner that parallels ISO 9000.

Of more recent interest is IEC 80001-1:2021[xxxv] This standard, titled "Application of risk management for IT-networks incorporating medical devices. Safety, effectiveness and security in the implementation and use of connected medical devices or connected health software" contains many definitions. The main definition for consideration here is that of the *"Medical IT Network"*, which was originally defined as *"an IT-NETWORK that incorporates at least one MEDICAL DEVICE"*, but now incorporates health software and health IT systems. An IT-NETWORK is defined as *"a system or systems composed of communicating nodes and transmission links to provide physically linked or wireless transmission between two or more specified communication nodes"* and is adapted from IEC 61907:2009, definition 3.1.1. The MEDICAL DEVICE definition is from the MDD. A hospital that connects even one medical device into its standard network (or, indeed, loads medical device software onto a non-medical device so connected or incorporates it into other systems) has thereby created a medical IT-Network. The bounds of this network are that of the responsible organisation[xxxvi] but do bring different responsibilities into play, as detailed in the standard. In particular the role of the medical IT-network risk manager is specified.This family of standards could stimulate cross disciplinary teams in hospitals, involving IT departments, informatics departments and clinical departments to establish quality systems for clinical computing. This would include: assurance of finance, planning of procurement and upgrades, and the monitoring of adequate support arrangements. Medical Physicists and Clinical Engineers would have an important role to play in these groups, particularly with regard to day to day running and relationships with device suppliers and the maintenance of a medical device asset register.

[xxxv] The previous edition, 80001-1:2010 is now withdrawn.
[xxxvi] Therefore a connection to the Internet does not render a network a medical IT-network.

Chapter 10 – Computers in a Clinical Environment

System Management

System management is often rendered "systems management" and is the management of the **information technology** (IT) systems in an enterprise[i]. This includes gathering requirements, purchasing equipment and software, distributing it to where it is to be used, configuring it, maintaining it with enhancement and service updates, setting up problem-handling processes, and determining whether objectives are being met. System management is usually under the overall responsibility of an enterprise's CIO.

Trends and issues in system management include:

- The total cost of ownership, which emphasises that updating and servicing equipment is likely to be a major cost
- The right balance of resources and control between centrally-managed and network-distributed systems
- The outsourcing of all or part of information systems and systems management
- Tactical versus strategic purchasing decisions
- The choices between proprietary, compatible, and Open Source software
- Exploitation of the Internet and Web interfaces
- Graphical user interfaces for controlling the information system
- Security management, including security for mobile device users
- Gathering requirements
- Purchasing equipment and software
- Distributing equipment and software to where it is to be used
- Setting up problem-handling processes
- Determining whether objectives are being met

We will now examine some of these further.

Configuring equipment and software

Configuration is the selection from a set of options in order to achieve the optimal system to serve the perceived need. A computer is a generalist machine, rather than a specific one[ii]. It is therefore originally set up to do as many things as possible well. But a fast graphical refresh rate in order to play computer games is of little use in an MRI suite, where rendering accuracy is more important. In configuration you decide which features are important, and promote them, and which are not, and demote them.

---

[i] in this case a hospital, not a starship
[ii] i.e. it does lots of things, driven by the software and hardware that is loaded into it.

Figure 57: A Configuration Menu for an Intel Graphics Card in a PC

Maintaining with enhancement and service updates

No computer program, including the OS, is ever complete. OSs in particular are so complex that while it may be theoretically possible to completely test them, it is not practical to do so. Software often therefore has three releases: alpha, beta and final.

An alpha release is not usually widely available and is normally only released to a select group of testers, often in-house. It is the "first draft" of the software and as such is generally unreliable and unfinished.

A beta release is more widely available and often to members of the public. The software may not be bug-free, but is expected to be nearly so. As with alpha users, there is no guarantee that things will work correctly but there is an expectation that discovered problems will be reported. Beta users tend to be those requiring a feature who are prepared to take the risk of something else not working, and those building add-ons.

The final release is the one that the normal user receives. This may still not be error-free and so the manufacturer will release patches for the software. The more complex the software the more frequent the patches: Microsoft bundle theirs and release them once a month.

Not all patches are fixes, though. Some will be enhancements – often features that were planned for release but not finished in time. Microsoft therefore classes its patches in two ways: security updates and regular updates. There is a third kind, the service pack, which is a bundling together of a lot of updates into one package. Hence Windows XP may be referred to as XP, XPSP1, XPSP2 or XPSP3, depending on the service pack applied.

It is not unusual for a medical device to allow security updates to be applied automatically but to disallow any others, including service packs. Manufacturers will generally test against service packs, but not regular updates, so service packs can be applied, but not immediately.

The total cost of ownership

Whilst it is often easy to calculate the cost of delivering a project once it is scheduled[iii], that is only one part of the equation and often overlooks the true cost of ownership. A much better method is Total **Cost of Ownership** (TCO). As an example, buying a car is the easy bit. Keeping this car on the road is the expensive part: no-one would budget to buy a car and not factor into the equation the tax, insurance and MoT[iv].

Classic business models built upon the failure of consumers to account for TCO are the razor and blade model, or (more recently) the printer and ink model. Both of these rely on low-profit initial purchases (the razor or printer) and higher-profit consumables (the blade or the ink) which are repeatedly purchased.

Gartner defines TCO as *"a comprehensive assessment of information technology (IT) or other costs across enterprise boundaries over time. For IT, TCO includes hardware and software acquisition, management and support, communications, end-user expenses and the opportunity cost of downtime, training and other productivity losses."[99]*

Total Cost of Ownership Calculator

Gray cells are calculated for you. You do not need to enter anything into them.

Cost per year	CRT monitor	LCD monitor	LCD monitor savings
Purchase cost	17.59	39.08	(21.50)
Cost of power	5.33	2.53	2.81
Cost of space	1,184.38	312.54	871.84
Visual task time	$6,260.83	$5,378.63	$882.21
Total	$7,450.55	$5,693.70	$1,756.85

Assumptions

		Unit of measurement
Product 1 [CRT monitor]		
Purchase price	150	Dollars
Power consumption	100	Watts per hour
Standby power	8	Watts
Width	16	Inches
Depth	18	Inches
Life expectancy	20000	Hours
Product 2 [LCD monitor]		
Purchase price	500	Dollars
Power consumption	47	Watts per hour
Standby power	5	Watts
Width	19	Inches
Depth	4	Inches
Life expectancy	30000	Hours

Indirect costs

Cost		Unit of measurement
Normal annual office hours	2,345	Hours per year
Average employment cost	14.71	Dollars per hour
Time spent using computer	33%	Percentage of working week
Time spent visual searching	15%	Percentage of computer use
Speed increase in visual tasks	25%	Percent by which speed is increased
Reading time	40%	Percentage of computer use
Speed increase in reading	10%	Percent by which speed is increased
Cost of electricity	6.63	Cents per 100 KW per hour
Average office cost	592.19	Dollars per sq. ft per year
% left on with power saving	10%	Percentage of computers
% left on without power saving	5%	Percentage of computers

Figure 58: Excel TCO Calculator[v]

Tactical versus strategic purchasing decisions

Strategic purchasing is the process of "*planning, implementing, evaluating, and controlling strategic and operating purchasing decisions for directing all activities of the purchasing function toward opportunities consistent with the firm's capabilities to achieve its long-term goals*"[100]. Tactical purchasing is typically a subset of activities and processes within the strategic purchasing approach. It focuses on operational purchasing requirements based on information from a limited environmental scan[101].

[iii] You know how many days it will take and how much those people cost, for example.

[iv] Actually, a lot do. But they shouldn't.

[v] downloadable from http://exceltemplates.net/calculator/total-cost-of-ownership-calculator/

Essentially, strategic actions are long-term: they may take a while to design, implement and achieve. Tactical actions are short-term. Ideally they should fit within the overall strategy, if there is one.

A simple example would be this: a strategic purchase is one that evaluates every network card on the market and decides which one will best serve the hospital over several years, especially when TCO is taken into account. A tactical purchase says I need one now and runs up to PC World to get it.

Virtual Environments

Computing has come a long way: from the Greek Antikythera analogue computer (Circa 100BCE) which was used for astronomical predictions, through the Babbage Analytical Engine (Circa 1840), Turing's Bombe (1940s), ENIAC (1945), the Apollo guidance computer (1960s) and into the PCs, tablets and embedded devices that we know today. In 1965 Gordon Moore stated Moore's law – the observation that the number of transistors in a dense integrated circuit doubles approximately every two years[vi].

Whilst this has increased computing power greatly, it has also increased the unwanted side-effects, most notably heat which thus requires more cooling, which involves moving parts (and in some systems water) and therefore increases reliability issues.

There has been a notable trend in recent years towards virtualising systems, especially for servers. In this, multiple servers are hosted on a single hardware platform, the load being distributed across all available processors.

The drivers of virtualisation are:

- CPU development has tended to lead software development
- Software applications were not using much of this new hardware power
- A single, over-resourced, physical machine can be divided into many smaller machines

This gives advantages of doing so, which include:

- Lower power consumption
- Less cooling required
- Less rack space
- Centralised administration
- Quick and efficient provisioning (just copy another **Virtual Machine** (VM))
- Easier backup and disaster recovery

[vi] Originally this was every year, but he revised it to 2 years in 1975

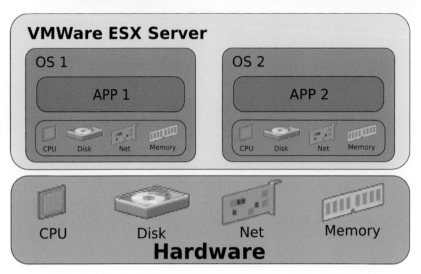

Figure 59: Schematic Representation of a Server Hosting Multiple Virtual Machines[102]

Multiple Apps may run under each OS

There are several vendors, such as VMware (ESXi), Microsoft (Hyper-V), Citrix (XenServer), Red Hat and KVM.

A virtual machine is not sized by providing it with more resources than it really needs, under the assumption that it'll never run out of resources and thus will work even better, as this wastes the very resources that we were trying to better utilise. Instead the "Goldilocks principle"[vii] is used, for if a VM has too little resource available then it has insufficient power to get things done whereas if it has too much resource then the unused vCPU still consumes host resource due to polling and unused memory.

A VM still requires storage, but this normally comes from the organisation's SAN, and thus can be added at any time (provided there's enough space on the SAN), it can be thick provisioned (like a physical server) or thin provisioned (it can use up to the amount requested).

VMs are not a one-size-fits-all solution, though. Some applications can't be virtualised (yet) due to high IO workloads (e.g. a Trust-wide SQL Server farm containing multiple databases) and some servers may have hardware plugins (dongles etc.) that they rely on.

Cloud Computing

Cloud computing is *a type of Internet-based computing that provides shared computer processing resources and data to computers and other devices on demand. It is a model for enabling ubiquitous, on-demand access to a shared pool of configurable computing resources (e.g., computer networks, servers, storage, applications and services), which can be rapidly provisioned and released with minimal management effort.*[103]

The main reasons to use the cloud are:

- System Prototyping and Evaluation
- Reduction of Costs - Saving Money
- Flexibility
- Universal access
- Up to date software
- Choice of software
- Potential to be greener and more economical

---

vii Not too much, not too little, but just right

118

There are three types of cloud:

- **Public Cloud:** a service provider makes resources, such as applications and storage, available to the general public over the Internet. Public cloud services may be free or offered on a pay-per-usage model.
- **Private cloud:** a type of cloud computing that delivers similar advantages to public cloud, including scalability and self-service, but through a proprietary architecture. Unlike public clouds, which deliver services to multiple organisations, a private cloud is dedicated to a single organisation.
- **Hybrid cloud:** a cloud computing environment which uses a mix of on-premises, private cloud and third-party, public cloud services with orchestration between the two platforms. By allowing workloads to move between private and public clouds as computing needs and costs change, hybrid clouds give businesses greater flexibility and more data deployment options.

There are five types of cloud service:

- **Platform as a Service** (PaaS): a cloud computing model that delivers applications over the internet. In a PaaS model, a cloud provider delivers hardware and software tools – usually those needed for application development – to its users as a service. A PaaS provider hosts the hardware and software on its own infrastructure. As a result, PaaS frees users from having to install in-house hardware and software to develop or run a new application.
- **Software as a Service** (SaaS): a third-party provider hosts software, removing the need for organisations to install and run applications on their own computers or in their own data centres. It eliminates the expense of hardware acquisition, provisioning and maintenance, as well as software licensing, installation and support.
- **Infrastructure as a Service** (IaaS): a third-party provider hosts hardware, software, servers, storage and other infrastructure components on behalf of its users. IaaS providers also host users' applications and handle tasks including system maintenance, backup and resiliency planning.
- **Data as a Service** (DaaS): the data is hosted, offering convenient and cost-effective solutions for customer- and client-oriented enterprises.
- **Backup as a Service** (BaaS): this may be used when an organisation has outgrown its legacy storage backup and would have to go through a costly upgrade, or lacks the resources for on-premises, high-level backup. Outsourcing backup and recovery to a provider can also keep data accessible or restorable from a remote location in case of an outage or failure.

These services can be visualised as follows: Consider a business responsible for selling shorts. There are a number of ways in which such a business might be set up, each relying on outside services to a greater or lesser extent:

In-house	Platform as a service	Software as a service	Infrastructure as a service	Data as a service	Backup as a service
Fabric	Fabric	Fabric	Fabric	Fabric	Fabric
Sewing machines	Sewing machines	Sewing machines	Sewing machines	Sewing machines	Sewing machines
Packaging and Shipping	Packaging and Shipping	Packaging and Shipping	Packaging and Shipping	Packaging and Shipping	Packaging and Shipping
Storage of stock	Storage of stock	Storage of stock	Storage of stock	Storage of stock	Storage of stock
Feedback & complaints	Feedback & complaints	Feedback & complaints	Feedback & complaints	Feedback & complaints	Feedback & complaints
Overflow storage	Overflow storage	Overflow storage	Overflow storage	Overflow storage	Overflow storage

Business manages
Vendor manages

Figure 60: Shorts as a Service[viii]

This maybe represented graphically as:

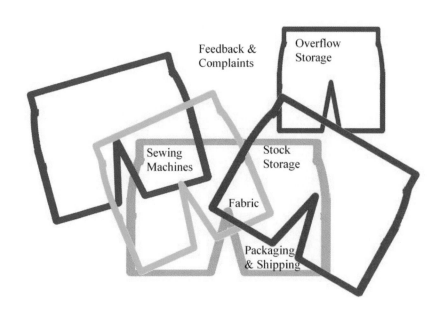

Figure 61: Shorts as a Service
The colours correspond to the borders in the above table

Security

Computers used clinically contain a great deal of sensitive data. It is also vitally important that they continue to function as intended. This section considers some of the issues with keeping such systems secure.

[viii] With thanks to Rachel O'Leary

Malware

Probably the most common security issue faced by NHS IT systems is that of viruses. Whilst the term "virus" is often used, it covers many different types of malicious software (or "malware") such as Trojans, worms, spyware and rootkits. There are two important features of such malware: it does something malicious and it can replicate itself, thereby passing from one device to another. The Trojan is probably the simplest of these. This is a piece of software that purports to perform some useful function (such as a system scan), which it may do. However, it also contains within it another program that performs the malicious action (such as seeking out passwords and emailing them). It may also copy itself to all other programs on the device, so that deleting the original program does not remove the Trojan from the system.

A worm is a program that seeks to exploit vulnerabilities in a device (or network), usually by probing certain access points or by appearing to be a "trusted" service. Having installed itself on the device ("infected" it), it is then able to activate its malicious element (the "payload").

Viruses may be resident or non-resident. Both types will have attached themselves to a legitimate executable program in order to be executed by the device. They will initiate (possibly complete) and then pass control to the host program. A non-resident virus will search for other files to infect and do so by copying its code into the new host (thereby replicating itself). A resident virus will not perform this action immediately, but will instead install itself into memory and attach itself to an operating system function, running each time this function is called. A virus scanner that fails to recognise such a virus may itself become the initiator, thereby causing each scanned file to become infected (via replication) as soon as the scan completes.

Virus technology is not new. John von Neumann described them in 1949[104], but it is the modern high level of connection in networks (and especially the Internet) that has seen the most widespread proliferation.

An anti-virus program will work in many ways, such as trapping unpermitted behaviour (see Data Loss Prevention, page 124), but the most common is the file scan. In this method, a file[ix] is examined byte by byte. The virus scanner has a set of patterns known as "virus definitions" that it is looking for. These are unique to the virus in question and are therefore not simply a few bytes long. In this way, Trojans and spyware can also be trapped. Once found, the scanner will perform some kind of corrective action, the most common of which are quarantine (moving the infected file somewhere else for further examination) or deletion. "Cleansing" the file is the removal of the virus but as viruses become more sophisticated this is not always successful.

In order for an anti-virus program to be successful, it must scan the files on the system. There are two main ways to do this: scheduled scanning and on-access scanning (frequently the two are combined).

On-access scanning scans files as and when they are accessed. In the case of an executable, this is just prior to its execution. Scheduled scanning scans the full system at a predefined time. On-access scanning is clearly the most secure, yet is not always applicable due to the processing overhead and time delay it introduces. This may not have any critical effect on entering figures into a spreadsheet, but is likely to in real-time control and acquisition software. For this reason most medical devices employ scheduled scanning, but it is therefore imperative that the scan is scheduled for a time when the device is operational[x].

Encryption

Assuming that the devices are secure and the connection is also, the next issue to address is that of interception. Data may be deliberately intercepted (via packet logging) or simply mislaid. In either case, the next level of security is encryption. Successful encryption means that only the authorised receiver can read the message.

[ix] Usually an executable program – but remember that many spreadsheets and word processing documents contain executable code in the form of macros.

[x] Scheduling the scan for 3am and switching the device off when the staff go home is poor planning.

Encryption is, of course, a very old science. It has gone from simple substitution ciphers[xi], through the complexity of the Enigma machine, to today's prime-number based techniques. The most common encryption is RSA developed by Rivest, Shamir and Adelman in 1978[105] and relies upon the difficulty of factoring into prime numbers. It works as follows:

- Let p and q be large prime numbers and let $N = pq$. Let e be a positive integer which has no factor in common with $(p-1)(q-1)$. Let d be a positive integer such that $ed - 1$ is divisible by $(p-1)(q-1)$.
- Let $f(x) = x^e \bmod N$, where $a \bmod N$ means "divide N into a and take the remainder."
- Let $g(x) = x^d \bmod N$.
- Use $f(x)$ for encryption, $g(x)$ for decryption.

[Clay Mathematics Institute[106]]

Therefore, in order to transmit a secure message only the numbers e and N are required. To decrypt the message, d is also required. This can be found by factoring N into p and q then solving the equation to find d. However, this factorisation would take millions of years using current knowledge and technology[xii][xiii].

A simpler method is **Pretty Good Privacy (**PGP) developed by Phil Zimmerman in 1991[107] and subsequently multiply revised. In this there is a single public key (published) which is used for encryption and a single private key which is used for decryption. In PGP a random key is first generated and is encrypted using the recipient's public key. The message is then encrypted using the generated (or "session") key. Both the encrypted key and the encrypted message are sent to the recipient. The recipient then decrypts the session key using their private key, with which they decrypt the message.

So far we have only considered data transmissions. Encryption can also be used on data "at rest", i.e. on a storage device. RSA encryption is therefore usable in this context, although PGP isn't (and the **Advanced Encryption Standard** (AES) is now more common for this purpose than RSA). There are two forms of encryption: hardware and software. Both use similar algorithms but the use of hardware encryption means that the resultant storage device is portable as it requires no software to be loaded in order to be used. A device may be fully encrypted[xiv] or filesystem-level encrypted, which just encrypts the storage being used (often the file names are in plain text, so be careful what you call your files). Devices may use multiple keys for different partitions, thereby not being fully compromised if one key is discovered.

Three final concepts must be considered before we move on from encryption: steganography, checksums and digital signatures. Steganography is a process of hiding files within other files, often at bit level – image files are therefore very suitable for this.

Checksums were originally developed due to the unreliability of electronic transmission. In the simplest form, the binary bits of each part of the message (which could be as small as a byte) were summed. If the result was odd, a bit with the value 1 would be added to the end of the message. If even, then the bit would be 0. Thus, by summing the entire message's bits, the result should always be even.

As an example, consider 9. As a 7-bit number this is 0001001. It has 2 1s, so the check digit is 0, giving 00010010. It is therefore vital to know whether you are using even or odd checksums (often called parity).

Extensions to this were developed in order to detect the corruption of multiple bits and also to correct simple errors. Developed to ensure the integrity of the message due to electronic failure, these techniques can also be used to detect tampering. (See "RAID", page 130).

[xi] Where each letter of the alphabet is exchanged for another. Decryption is a simple matter of reversing the substitution.
[xii] It is not worth beginning to speculate on the effect of a mathematician discovering a fast factorisation method.
[xiii] See https://sites.math.washington.edu/~morrow/336_09/papers/Yevgeny.pdf for a good description of how it all works
[xiv] i.e. the entire storage, sometimes including the master boot record

A full-file checksum is commonly used to ensure the reliable transmission of the file (e.g. from memory stick to PC) and is calculated using a hashing function. *"The most common checksums are MD5 and SHA-1, but both have been found to have vulnerabilities. This means that malicious tampering can lead to two different files having the same computed hash. Due to these security concerns, the newer SHA-2 is considered the best cryptographic hash function since no attack has been demonstrated on it as of yet"*[108]. A checksum is calculated by the transmitting (or source) system and also by the receiving (or destination) system and compared. If they are the same, then the file is presumed to have been transferred without corruption.

A simple checksum example is the bank card. If you write out the 10-digit number, then replace every other number (starting with the first) with twice its value, then sum all the resultant digits[xv], you get a multiple of ten. Thus a website can quickly verify that the card number is in a valid form before contacting the card issuer for verification. The clever bit in this method is in doubling every other digit, because the most common error in typing in a string of numbers is transposition, which this catches. Just adding the digits wouldn't do this.[109]

Digital signatures verify where the information received is from. It uses a similar asymmetric cryptography technique to PGP, in that a message is signed (encrypted) using a public key and verified (decrypted) using a private key. A more complex version also uses the message, thereby demonstrating (in a similar fashion to checksums) that the message has not been altered. A valid digital signature provides three assurances: the message was created by a known sender, the sender cannot deny having sent the message, and the message was not altered in transit.

Digital signatures are commonly used for software distribution, financial transactions, contract management software, and in other cases where it is important to detect forgery or tampering. They are also often used to implement electronic signatures[xvi]. In many countries, including the United States, Algeria, Turkey, India, Brazil, Indonesia, Mexico, Saudi Arabia, Uruguay, Switzerland and in the European Union, electronic signatures have legal significance.

Access Control
Having secure messaging and secure storage, we can now consider further access controls on a server. There are two methods to consider here: direct (shared filesystem) and remote (or terminal). Both require a system of authentication.

For filesystem access (such as to a shared folder) the server administrator will grant permission for the folder[xvii] (and subfolders) to be accessed by specific users. This may be individually, or by groups. The latter is simpler to maintain, but takes longer to set up. A mixture of methods is possible. Permissions on a folder include permission to read, to write, to delete and to create/delete subfolders – all of which may be granted or denied individually. It is also possible to grant/deny these permissions on individual files. Where this is not done, files inherit the permissions of the folder that contains them.

[xv] Remember that if you had "8" this was doubled to "16" and you now have "7" as this is "1+6"
[xvi] A broader term that refers to any electronic data that carries the intent of a signature, but not all electronic signatures use digital signatures
[xvii] Or directory, on UNIX and Linux servers.

Figure 62: Access Control under Windows 7

Direct access will usually be achieved by mounting the server's shared folder as a remote folder on the accessing device. If there are insufficient privileges, then mounting will fail.

Remote access is achieved through a separate program, such as Telnet, **Secure Socket Layer** (SSL) or **Remote Desktop Protocol** (RDP). For all of these, the server[xviii] must be configured to accept such connections and will need to be verified via a username/password combination. Telnet is the most trusting of the three and SSL the most secure, but once they are set up the experience of using them is very similar[xix].

The Human Factor

We will now consider the security of the data itself. **Data Loss Prevention** (DLP) is of particular interest to NHS organisations as the movement and transfer of patient-identifiable data is tightly controlled.

DLP may take many forms: system-wide policies can be applied in which no data can be written to removable devices (or restricted to encrypted ones); emails may be examined to determine if they contain patient-identifiable information (usually via keyword searches); all emails to non-NHS addresses may be encrypted on departure; firewall rules may permit data to be sent from certain devices only at specified times. Sadly, the most common cause of data loss in the NHS is human error. Technology merely reduces this.

One useful such technology is the NHSmail service, which is a secure service. It is authorised for sending sensitive information, such as clinical data, between NHSmail and:

- NHSmail addresses (i.e. from an *.nhs.net or *.hscic.gov.uk account to an *.nhs.net or *.hscic.gov.uk account)
- Government secure email domains (between *.nhs.net and *.gsi.gov.uk, *.gse.gov.uk and *.gsx.gov.uk)
- Police National Network/Criminal Justice Services secure email domains (between *.nhs.net and *.pnn.police.uk, *.cjsm.net)

[xviii] Which may be an individual PC.

[xix] Although beware versions – you may have to set one tunnel up differently to another, depending on what is at the other end.

- Ministry of Defence secure email domains (*.mod.uk and *.mod.gov.uk).
- Local Government/Social Services secure email domains (*.nhs.net and *.gcsx.gov.uk)

Sensitive data may be exchanged outside of the above secure domains, using the NHSmail encryption tool.

Keeping it fresh

Security systems cannot remain static as attempts to break them do not. We have already mentioned password complexity and expiry as being one method of change. The others of interest here are virus signatures and operating system patches.

Virus signatures generally do not change. However, new viruses continually appear – either as a new variant on an old idea or in response to a new security flaw being discovered. Therefore virus signature files need to be kept up-to-date. In an enterprise, this will generally be done by a local update server. This communicates with the main online repository (e.g. Sophos) and then distributes the updates on a regular basis (usually daily) around the enterprise. Using such a system means that the updates only have to be downloaded once, thus reducing Internet traffic and potential delays.

The second (and better) way of combating security flaws in an operating system is to repair them. This is usually done via an update patch to the OS itself (discussed on page 115). Again, enterprise-wide this is best achieved via an update server. The patches can then be pushed out to the IT estate and installed at the correct time – usually on shut-down. There are, of course, potential issues with this approach for medical devices which may never be shut down or may not have a sufficiently predictable "down time" that can be used.

Sadly, in February 2018 the **Public Accounts Committee** (PAC) were informed that of 200 Trusts assessed for cyber security vulnerabilities, none met the standards set by inspectors – many failing purely on patching, which was what the (then) recent WannaCry[xx] attack had exploited[110].

Group Policy Object

Group Policy is a feature of the Microsoft Windows family of operating systems from NT upwards that controls the working environment of user accounts and computer accounts. Group Policy provides the centralised management and configuration of operating systems, applications, and users' settings in an Active Directory environment.

Group Policy in part controls what users can and cannot do on a computer system, for example: to enforce a password complexity policy that prevents users from choosing an overly simple password, to allow or prevent unidentified users from remote computers to connect to a network share, to block access to the Windows Task Manager or to restrict access to certain folders. A set of such configurations is called a **Group Policy Object** (GPO).

Group Policy Objects are processed in the following order from top to bottom:

1. Local - Any settings in the computer's local policy. Prior to Windows Vista, there was only one local group policy stored per computer. Windows Vista and later Windows versions allow individual group policies per user account.
2. Site - Any Group Policies associated with the Active Directory site in which the computer resides. (An Active Directory site is a logical grouping of computers, intended to facilitate management of those computers based on their physical proximity.) If multiple policies are linked to a site, they are processed in the order set by the administrator.
3. Domain - Any Group Policies associated with the Windows domain in which the computer resides. If multiple policies are linked to a domain, they are processed in the order set by the administrator.

[xx] WannaCry started on May 12 2017 and is thought to have affected 81 Trusts and almost 600 GP surgeries, according to the National Audit Office.

4.   Organizational Unit - Group policies assigned to the Active Directory **organizational unit** (OU) in which the computer or user are placed. (OUs are logical units that help with organising and managing a group of users, computers or other Active Directory objects.) If multiple policies are linked to an OU, they are processed in the order set by the administrator.

The Group Policy settings applied to a given computer or user are known as the **Resultant Set of Policy** (RSoP). RSoP information may be displayed for both computers and users using the *gpresult* command.

Microsoft (R) Windows (R) XP Operating System Group Policy Result tool v2.0

Created On 14/02/2014 at 17:57:40

RSOP results for UCLH\pganney on PCLCMG40034 : Logging Mode

OS Type: Microsoft Windows XP Professional
OS Configuration: Member Workstation
OS Version: 5.1.2600
Domain Name: UCLH
Domain Type: Windows 2000
Site Name: UCH-MIDDX
Roaming Profile:
Local Profile: D:\Personal Data\pganney
Connected over a slow link?: No

COMPUTER SETTINGS

  CN=PCLCMG40034,OU=Workstations,OU=Standard,OU=Devices,DC=xuclh,DC=nhs,DC=uk
  Last time Group Policy was applied: 14/02/2014 at 16:19:38
  Group Policy was applied from: UADDC103.xuclh.nhs.uk
  Group Policy slow link threshold: 500 kbps

  Applied Group Policy Objects

    GPO_Computers_XPSP2_Off2003
    Local Group Policy

  The computer is a part of the following security groups:

    BUILTIN\Administrators
    Everyone

USER SETTINGS

  CN=Ganney\,Paul,OU=Users,OU=Standard,OU=UCLH Users,DC=xuclh,DC=nhs,DC=uk
  Last time Group Policy was applied: 14/02/2014 at 16:30:58

```
Group Policy was applied from:        UADDC103.xuclh.nhs.uk
Group Policy slow link threshold:   500 kbps


Applied Group Policy Objects
-----------------------------
    GPO_Personal_May2012


The following GPOs were not applied because they were filtered out
------------------------------------------------------------------
    GPO_NuclearMedicineScript
        Filtering:  Denied (Security)


The user is a part of the following security groups:
----------------------------------------------------
    Domain Users
    Everyone
    BUILTIN\Users
    NT AUTHORITY\INTERACTIVE
    NT AUTHORITY\Authenticated Users
    LOCAL
    IM&T (Trust Users)
    MPB - Computing & Instrumentation staff
```

Figure 63: Part of a gpresult for a Computer when running Windows XP

A policy setting inside a hierarchical structure is ordinarily passed from parent to children, and from children to grandchildren, and so forth. This is termed inheritance. It can be blocked or enforced to control what policies are applied at each level. If a higher level administrator (enterprise administrator) creates a policy that has inheritance blocked by a lower level administrator (domain administrator), this policy will still be processed.

For example, to prevent the user from being able to save desktop settings on exit, right click on the Don't save settings at exit policy setting (see Figure 64) and select the Properties command from the context menu. To set such a policy, select the Enabled radio button and click OK (see Figure 65). The Disabled option is used to turn off a policy that was applied at a higher level. For example, suppose that the domain group policy prevented anyone from saving desktop settings on exit, but "disable" here allows you to do this.

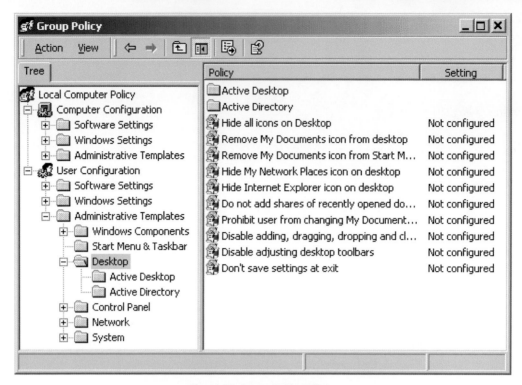

Figure 64: Group Policy Editor

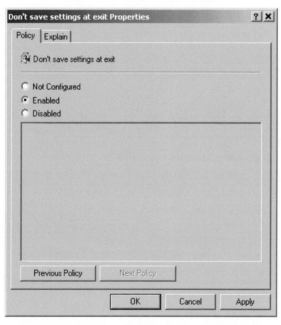

Figure 65: The Dialog for Altering a Group Policy Object

Testing

We have already covered software testing (page 80). The principles described there apply equally to configuration and system testing. It should be noted, though, that such testing is very unlikely to be white-box.

Disaster Recovery

A reliable data centre, be it for a web presence, a clinical database or a document repository requires resilience to be built into the design. As with security, there are many ways of achieving this and the best designs will incorporate a mixture of these. In this section we consider four such techniques.

Replication

Replication, either of a server or a database (or both) is what the name implies: a copy exists of the server/data enabling it to be switched to in the event of a failure in the primary system. There are two main ways of achieving this, and the required uptime of the system determines which is the most appropriate. The simplest one to achieve is a copy, taken at a specified time, to the secondary system. The two systems are therefore only ever briefly synchronised and in the event of a system failure bringing the secondary system on line means that the data will be at worst out-of-date by the time interval between copying. Replication of this form is usually overnight (thereby utilising less busy periods for systems) meaning that the copy is at worst nearly 24 hours out-of-date. If changes to the system have been logged, then these may be run against the secondary system before bringing it on-line, but this will lengthen the time taken to do so.

The most common use of this form of replication is in data repositories (covered in Hospital Information Systems on page 41), thereby removing some of the workload from the primary system and improving its reliability (and response time).

The second method of replication is synchronised: that is, both copies are exactly the same at all times. There are two primary ways of achieving this. The simplest is a data splitter: all changes sent to the primary system are also sent to the secondary (see HL7 for details on messaging, page 45). This is clearly the best method when the system receives changes via an interface (which may be from an input screen or from a medical device) as the primary system only has to process the incoming message and the work of replication is external to it (e.g. in an interface engine)[xxi]. The second is where every change to the primary system is transmitted to the secondary for it to implement. This introduces a processing overhead on the primary system, especially if it has to also receive acknowledgement that the change has been applied to the secondary system. As this method introduces a messaging system, the system could instead be designed to use the first method described.

The most basic (and therefore most common) method of replication, though, is the backup. This is simply a copy of the system (or a part of it) taken at a specified time, usually onto removable media (for high volumes, usually tape). As such backups are generally out-of-hours and unattended, systems that exceed the capacity of the media are backed up in portions, a different portion each night.

Whilst a backup enables a quick restore of lost or corrupted data (and simplifies system rebuilds in the case of major failure), data errors are usually not so swiftly noticed and may therefore also exist on the backup. The **Grandfather-Father-Son** (GFS) backup rotation system was developed to reduce the effect of such errors. In this, three tapes are deployed: on day one, tape 1 is used. On day 2, tape 2 is used and on day 3 tape 3 is used. On day 4 tape 1 is re-used and so on, meaning that there are always three generations (hence the name) of backup. Most backup regimes are variants on the GFS scheme and may include a different tape for each day of the week, 52 tapes (e.g. every Wednesday) also rotated or 12 tapes (e.g. every first Wednesday). In this way data errors tracing back as far as a year may be corrected.

Archiving

Despite the massive increases in storage capacity in recent years, medical imaging has also advanced and thus produces even larger data sets. It has been estimated that 80% of PACS images are never viewed again. However, as a reliable method for identifying those 80% has not yet been achieved, all images must be kept, but keeping them

---

[xxi] It is often postulated that giving the primary and secondary systems the same IP address will also achieve this. It is left as an exercise to determine whether or not this is a good idea.

online (on expensive storage) is not a sensible option. Thus old images are generally archived onto removable media[xxii] (again, tape is usual) or onto a slower, less expensive system and the original data deleted to free up space. There are several algorithms for identifying data suitable for archiving, but the most common is based on age: not the age of the data, but the time since it was last accessed. In order to implement such a system it is therefore imperative that each access updates the record, either in the database (for single items) or by the operating system (in the case of files).

Resilience using RAID

Probably the most common type of resilience, especially on a server, is **Redundant Array of Inexpensive Discs** (RAID)[xxiii]. There are several forms of RAID and we consider two (levels 1 and 5) here. RAID level 1 is a simple disc image, as per replication above – only in real-time. The replication is handled by the RAID controller[xxiv] which writes any information to both discs simultaneously. If one disc fails, then the other can be used to keep the system operational. The failed disc may then be replaced[xxv] and the RAID controller builds the new disc into a copy of the current primary over a period of time, depending on the amount of data held and the processing load.

Other forms of RAID do not replicate the data directly, but spread it across several discs instead, adding in some error correction as well. The form of spreading (known as "striping") and the type of error correction are different for each level of RAID.

RAID 5 uses block-level striping and parity data, spread across all discs in the array. In all disc storage, the disc is divided up into a set of blocks, a block being the smallest unit of addressable storage. A file will therefore occupy at least one block, even if the file itself is only one byte in size. A read or write operation on a disc will read or write a set of blocks. In RAID 5 these blocks are spread across several discs, with parity data stored on another one (see Figure 66). Thus RAID 5 always requires a minimum of three discs to implement.

RAID 5

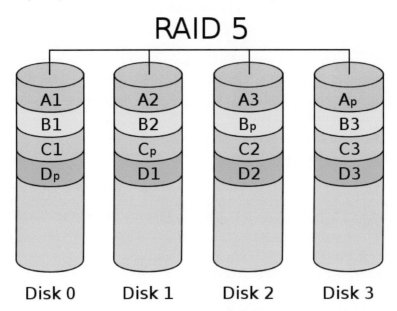

Figure 66: Diagram of a RAID 5 Setup[111]

Each letter represents the group of blocks in the respective parity block (a stripe)

[xxii] There may be several "layers" of such storage, each slower to access than the previous, eventually reaching a removable media layer

[xxiii] "I" is sometimes rendered "Independent".

[xxiv] A disc controller with additional functionality.

[xxv] Often without halting the system – known as "hot swapping".

Parity, which we met earlier, is a computer science technique for reducing data corruption. It was originally designed for data transmission and consisted of adding an extra bit to the data[xxvi]. This extra bit forced the sum of the bits to be odd (odd parity) or even (even parity). It was added at transmission and checked at reception (although this would only detect one error)[xxvii]. More complex forms used more bits which enabled the data not just to be better checked, but also to be corrected. Such codes are known as Hamming codes. The parity used within RAID 5 not only checks that the data is correct, but also enables it to be re-built, should a disc fail and have to be replaced[xxviii]. As a RAID controller can keep a system operational even when a disc has failed, so much so that users may not notice, it is therefore imperative to monitor such clusters as one failure may be easily fixed but two may be catastrophic.

In the figure, the distribution of the blocks and the parity can clearly be seen. Distributing the parity blocks distributes the load across all the discs, as this is where bottlenecks may appear (to read blocks B3 to C1, for example, also requires two parity blocks to be read – in this case each disc only has one read operation to perform). RAID 5 has found favour as it is viewed as the best cost-effective option providing both good performance and good redundancy. As write operations can be slow, RAID 5 is a good choice for a database that is heavily read-oriented, such as image review or clinical look-up.

Traditionally computer systems and servers have stored operating systems and data on their own dedicated disc drives. With the data requirements expanding it has now become more common to have separate large data stores using NAS or SAN technology. These differ in their network connectivity but both rely on RAID for resilience. NAS uses TCP/IP connections and SANs use Fibre Channel connections.

Business Continuity
The other half of **Disaster Recovery** (DR) is **Business Continuity** (BC): while the scientists and engineers are recovering from the disaster and restoring service, how does the business continue (if at all)? A good BC plan will firstly describe downtime procedures.

From these downtime procedures it is possible to work out how long the service/organisation can survive for. This then informs the DR plan. A service that can survive for a week needs little additional architecture. A service that can only tolerate 30 minutes requires redundant spares to be on-site. If it can only tolerate 5 minutes then hot-swaps are required. Less than a minute's tolerance requires a duplicate fail-over system to be running.

We looked at risk analysis earlier (page 51) and that should be the core of the DR and BC plans: what can go wrong (including infrastructure such as power and transport – human as well as data) and how much impact will it have.

[xxvi] An alternative was to use one of the 8 bits in each byte for parity. Hence ASCII only uses 7 bits and simple integers often only have a range of 0 to 127.
[xxvii] For a 7-digit binary number, 3 bits are required to check for all possible errors.
[xxviii] Therefore a failed disc can be ignored as the data on it can be computed in real time by the RAID controller.

Chapter 11 – Safety Management of Medical Devices

The advancement of technology has meant that the nature of medical devices has changed radically. Where previously they were solely hardware with no ability to collect data on the patient that they were connected to they are now very computer based with the ability to network to information systems within the healthcare organisation. So when we consider safety management of medical devices the issues are not solely hardware-related but are now the same problems encountered by PCs on networks. There are a number of standards and regulations that give guidance on how the safety issues should be addressed and so that is a good place to start.

Regulations

We met the MDD in Chapter 9. It includes a number of **Essential Requirements** (ER) for safety and performance which are given the following headings:

- Chemical, Physical and Biological Properties
- Infection and Microbial Contamination
- Construction and Environmental Properties
- Devices with a Measuring Function
- Protection Against Radiation
- Requirements for Medical Devices Connected to or Equipped with an Energy Source
- Information Supplied by the Manufacturer

In Annex IX there are rules to classify the equipment according to risk. The four possibilities are:

- CLASS I – LOW
- CLASS IIa – MEDIUM (Low Risk)
- CLASS IIb – MEDIUM (High Risk)
- CLASS III – HIGH RISK

The risk level determines the route that has to be followed to CE marking which is essential for the device to be put on the market.

In 2010 an amendment was introduced that explicitly said that software in its own right can be classified as a medical device[i]. It also introduced such terms as **Standalone Medical Device** (SaMD) which refers to software that is not part of a medical device but can work in conjunction with such devices. On occasions software may also be an accessory to a Medical Device.

Within the UK it is the **Medicines and Healthcare Regulatory Agency** (MHRA) that is the competent authority responsible for enforcing the MDD\MDR through law.

Standards

We have already met many standards, but three more deserve mention here:

- 80601-2-x – *Medical Electrical Equipment*, a set of standards with dates between 2009 and 2015. For example, *ISO 80601-2-61:2011 Medical electrical equipment - Part 2-61: Particular requirements for basic safety and essential performance of pulse oximeter equipment.*
- 62353:2014 - *Medical electrical equipment. Recurrent test and test after repair of medical electrical equipment*
- 82304-1:2016 *Health Software.* For example, *IEC 82304-1:2016 applies to the safety and security of health software products designed to operate on general computing platforms and intended to be placed on the market without dedicated hardware, and its primary focus is on the requirements for manufacturers. It*

---

[i] Directive 2007/47/EC

covers the entire lifecycle including design, development, validation, installation, maintenance, and disposal of health software products.[112]

The effects of these standards on software medical devices are that:

- They are formally recognised in the MDD – 2007 revision.

- Software as a Medical Device and Standalone software come into the scope of the standards.

- They are related to IEC 60601 by the **Programmable Electrical Medical System** (PEMS) and **Programmable Electrical Sub System** (PESS) clauses. (NB Software\Firmware is a PESS).

- PACS Workstations are classified as Medical Devices.

- PACS Servers are generally not classified as a medical device because they only store data – instead they are classified as **Medical Device Data Systems (**MDDS). A MDDS can still be classified as Class I MD – but such regulation is much relaxed even by FDA.

- Close potential loophole for software that should be classified MD but supplier tries to avoid CE or FDA 510k process.

- IEC 62304 introduced to aid approval process.

- Software is classified by risk levels:

    - A – Low (No risk of patient death)

    - B- Medium (May cause death)

    - C – High (Would cause death)

- IEC 82304 – Widens scope to include health software.

The Effect of Electricity on the Body and Protection Against Electric Shocks

The neuro-muscular impact of an electric shock depends on the current density, frequency and duration of the shock and the particular neuro-muscular system involved.

For 50Hz current passing between the hands the following ascending scale of effects are:

- 1 mA – Perception

- 10 mA – Can't let go

- 100 mA – Severe pain and interference to the heart and chest function

- 1 A – Sustained heart contraction

Effects start to diminish at frequencies above 100KHz.

Exceptionally high currents passing through the body cause tissue heating, the extent of which depends on the local current and resistance because:

Power = Voltage (V) * Current (I) but

Voltage = Resistance (R) * Current (I) so

Power = R * I * I or R * I^2

Cutting (using diathermy), Coagulation and Physiotherapy Ultrasound are controlled uses of this effect.

Direct or very low frequency currents (less than 0.1Hz) are conducted as ionic[ii] currents which can cause ulcerations of the skin that are slow to heal but are used deliberately in some hair removal techniques.

The UK mains supply is 230V 50Hz. The primary hazard when dealing with mains is that the line connection is seeking a route to earth by any means. The most effective protection against electrocution is dry skin and the ability to pull away. Hospital patients have both of these removed due to low impedance skin connections and sedatives. **Protective Earthing** (PE) is a common method used to reduce electrical hazards by providing a low resistance path to earth in the case of a fault. Double insulated equipment does not require a safety earth because no mains parts are accessible.

In many cases there are leakage currents present even when equipment is operating normally, the potential dangers of which are reduced by use of a PE.

There are three main classifications for Medical Equipment to indicate protection against electric shock:

- Class 1 equipment relies on a protective earth.

- Class 2 equipment relies on double layers of insulation.

- Class 3 equipment is internally powered below the **Safety Extra Low Voltage** (SELV) level of 50 VAC.

These classifications are further subdivided by the degree of protection for patient applied parts:

- Type B equipment has a patient part which may have a low impedance path to earth

- Type BF equipment has a floating type patient part that has a high impedance path to earth using devices such as a transformer.

- Type CF equipment is similar to BF but has much lower allowed levels of leakage that are deemed safe even when connected directly to the heart.

Leakage Current (mA)	Type B		Type BF		Type CF	
	NC	SFC	NC	SFC	NC	SFC
Earth	0.5	1	0.5	1	0.5	1
Enclosure	0.1	0.5	0.1	0.5	0.1	0.5
Patient	0.1	0.5	0.1	0.5	0.01	0.05

Figure 67: Table Showing the Maximum Allowed Leakage Current

NC = Normal Condition, SFC = Single Fault Condition

Medical Device Management
The MHRA document "Medical Device Management" (2014) replaced the "Device Bulletin" 2006 (05) published in November 2006.

Medical device management covers:

- Systems of management for medical equipment

- Acquisition of medical equipment

[ii] *"Relating to, composed of, or using ions."*; *"Often contrasted with covalent"* – Oxford dictionary online

- Maintenance and repair
- Decontamination
- Removal from service

All re-useable medical equipment is subject to regular preventative maintenance to comply with manufacturer guidelines as a minimum. This can be carried out by either the local hospital team or by manufacturers or by a third party, but when it is handled locally it is important that appropriate training is be given to the team. The availability of this is checked during procurement by use of a **Pre-Purchase Questionnaire** (PPQ).

Custom made safety testers are available that will carry out the required measurements for:

- Earth Continuity
- Insulation Resistance
- Earth Leakage
- Enclosure Leakage
- Patient Leakage

A lot of medical equipment such as CT, MR and ultrasound are now based on Windows Operating Systems. As all safety testers interrupt the mains supply to give a **Single Fault Condition** (SFC), there is the danger of damage to a PC hard disk and therefore the medical equipment. This may lead to the need for the system to be re-installed.

The solution to this problem is to make sure that the medical equipment is powered down between tests. In addition most testers have a manual mode. There is also a new generation of testers that will correctly handle PC based systems.

An additional difficulty is that testers are only suitable for equipment with a mains plug up to a maximum rating for current. Unfortunately one of these:

Figure 68: A UK Medical Safety Tester

Can't test one of these:

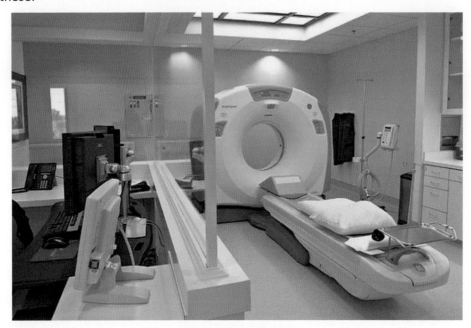

Figure 69: A CT Scanner[iii]

In the past all electrical safety testers were setup to test to IEC 60601 values, but now there is a new generation that tests to IEC 62353:2008[iv] which offers a change of emphasis from the type testing of IEC 60601 and a reduced potential for the testing to damage the equipment.

The next challenge is to locate the medical devices in question. It would be foolish to wander around a large hospital hoping to trip over the particular piece of equipment required by today's maintenance schedule. Instead we use technology such as WiFi enabled tags to offer a real-time display of the location of tagged devices overlaid onto building floor plans. See "Device tracking systems" (page 42) for an analysis of the pros and cons of a variety of locating technology.

[iii] 1weezie23, 2010. Used under GNU license via Wikimedia Commons
[iv] Medical Electrical Equipment, Recurrent Test and Test After Repair of Medical Electrical Equipment

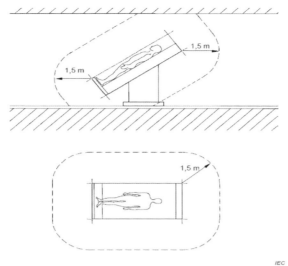

Figure 70: The Patient Environment[113]

Figure 70 illustrates the patient environment, within which all equipment must comply with the requirements for safety of medical equipment. The problem is that not all equipment is built to comply with IEC 60601-1; for example would a standard PC be allowed to be used for data gathering from medical equipment? The answer is yes providing that adequate precautions are taken to ensure that the PC is made to meet the relevant safety standards.

This may be achieved by:

- Connecting the PC mains supply via a medical grade isolation transformer. If the PC is networked then a medical grade LAN isolator is required as well. All this has the effect of reducing the earth, enclosure and patient leakage to safe levels as defined in IEC60601-1.

- Using medical grade isolators on the signal connections. A whole range of these are now available.

- Using a medical grade PC. These are now widely available from a number of suppliers.

A **Medical Electrical System** (MES) is a collection of equipment both medical and non-medical that interconnects via signal connections.

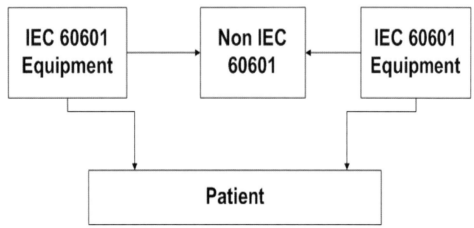

Figure 71: A Medical Electrical System

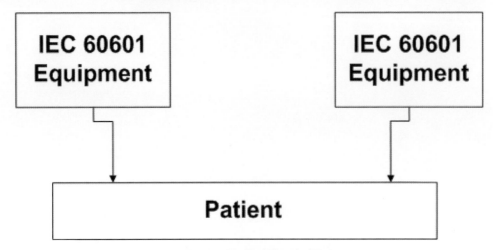

Figure 72: Not a Medical Electrical System

Two pieces of equipment connected solely through a patient does not constitute a Medical Electrical System

When equipment is connected in this way, even when it is all properly certified medical electrical equipment there is a possibility that dangerous levels of enclosure leakage may be present. In addition it is common to connect all the parts using a **Multiple Power Socket Outlet** (MPSO). If precautions are not taken other equipment may be connected into this MPSO and safety may be compromised.

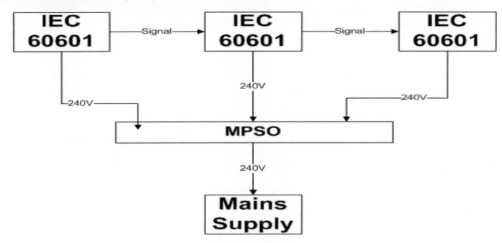

Figure 73: Use of a MPSO in a MES

Steps must be taken to ensure that the system is safe:

- Each individual part of the system must pass a full Medical Electrical Safety Test.

- The combined earth leakage must be measured under normal conditions. The result should not exceed 0.5mA

- The protective earth to each element of the system must be broken one at a time and the enclosure leakage measured on each part of the system. The result should not exceed 0.5mA

- The earth resistance for each system element back to the MPSO plug must be measured. The result should not exceed 0.4Ω

When considering a MES note that there is a change in the allowable earth resistance under normal conditions (0.1Ω to 0.4Ω) but not the earth leakage (0.5mA). The MPSO must either be covered to prevent the connection of unwanted items without the aid of a tool or must use a non-standard connector.

138

Networked Medical Devices

In the past patient information was hand written and stored in physical notes. Now we have:

- **Admission, Discharge and Transfer** (ADT) systems.

- PACS for medical images.

- **Clinical Information Systems** (CIS) for Patient Charts.

- A variety of archiving systems.

These combine to form the EPR and require medical devices to be networked.

As previously mentioned many current medical devices are based on Windows operating systems and more importantly older Windows OS's such as 2000 and XP. Due to the extensive validation of a medical device, patches and security updates cannot be installed in real time and in the majority of cases anti-virus software is not present and cannot be installed. This therefore presents a real security issue.

We deal with this by implementing measures to mitigate the risk, such as internal firewalls to segregate medical devices and implementing the 80001 series of standards (see chapter 9).

This work enables us to deliver the advantages of such systems:

- Better record keeping through central archiving.

- Greater patient safety through central admin of critical systems such as drug libraries for infusion devices.

But it does bring one major disadvantage: if security is not handled effectively, major parts of the hospital may be forced to close, such as A&E, as modern healthcare is very dependent on the networked medical device and without the network care cannot be adequately delivered.[v]

---

[v] In October 2016, several Lincolnshire hospitals were forced to cancel planned operations due to a computer virus (www.bbc.com/news/uk-england-humber-37822084, accessed August 2022)

Chapter 12 – Project management

Project Management (PM) is the process and activity of planning, organising, motivating, and controlling resources to achieve specific goals. A project is a temporary endeavour designed to produce a unique product, service or result with a defined beginning and end (usually time-constrained, and often constrained by funding or deliverables), undertaken to meet unique goals and objectives, typically to bring about beneficial change or added value. The temporary nature of projects stands in contrast with business as usual (or operations), which are repetitive, permanent, or semi-permanent functional activities to produce products or services. In practice, the management of these two systems is often quite different, and as such requires the development of distinct technical skills and management strategies.

The primary challenge of PM is to achieve all of the project goals and objectives while honouring the preconceived constraints. The primary constraints are scope, time, quality and budget. The secondary —and more ambitious— challenge is to optimise the allocation of necessary inputs and integrate them to meet pre-defined objectives.

PM allows you to work out WHAT problem you need to solve, whereas software development methods tell you HOW to build software. It is too often assumed that building software is the solution.

Writing a piece of software is not a project. Writing a piece of software to solve a specific problem, putting it into practice and keeping it running; that's a project[i].

Project management also helps to create a 'controlled development environment', which (along with quality management) is important for activities that can have risk implications such as implementing novel algorithms, automating activities and situations involving patient safety.

There are many project management methodologies around, but the NHS has focussed largely on **PRojects IN Controlled Environments** (PRINCE) 2, which was developed by the UK Government although it is used widely in the private sector. It attempts to ensure:

- An organised and controlled start i.e. organise and plan things properly before leaping in
- An organised and controlled middle i.e. when the project has started, make sure it continues to be organised and controlled
- An organised and controlled end i.e. when you've got what you want and the project has finished, tidy up the loose ends

A PRINCE 2 project progresses through many stages (you may spot a similarity with software lifecycle – especially Waterfall – here) in order to meet its goal. Management of a PRINCE 2-controlled project is done by two bodies: a **Project Board** (PB) and a **Project Team** (PT). The PB steers the project and is responsible for the resourcing of it, the PT delivers the project. A **Project Manager** (PM) is responsible for the day-to-day running of the project and sits on both bodies, reporting to the PB and managing the PT. The PM will create regular status reports for the PB, describing progress made, obstacles to be overcome and the use of resources to date (especially finance), often using a simple traffic-light system (or **Red-Amber-Green** (RAG) status) to provide an at-a-glance overview of the various components. Obstacles that cannot be overcome or other variations to the project plan are managed as exceptions and the PM will present an exception report to the PB for approval. A PM would normally be a certified PRINCE 2 Practitioner.

---

[i] Actually it's not as "keeping it running" should be **Business As Usual** (BAU) but for the purposes of this chapter, we'll pretend it is.

Starting Off

To initiate a project, a **Project Initiation Document** (PID) is required. This defines the scope of the project: the timescales, the purpose, the constraints and the benefits. It may also contain the maintenance methodology and eventual decommissioning plan. It should be written and approved by the project sponsors[ii] before work commences. That does not mean that exploratory work cannot be undertaken in advance, including prototyping, but a PID should be in place prior to the detailed work on the project commencing.

A PID provides a useful tool for both management and for those working on the project, clarifying what is needed as well as identifying possible issues before they arise. It needs to identify the requirements of the software, the risks and benefits as well as the staff, skills and time needed. The resulting paperwork may be as little as one page of A4.

Software development in a Medical Physics/Clinical Engineering environment needs to sit within a project framework and, as the problems are usually novel, there may be implications for service activities and there could also be significant safety issues involved. PM should prompt some introspection to decide whether the available in-house skills and resources are adequate to meet the demands of the project. The PID forms the basis of the management decision to actually undertake the project and put resources behind it (as well as the agreement from clinical sponsors that this is indeed what is being asked for). It may be that the project never progresses beyond this stage because defining the project shows it is too risky, too expensive, or just isn't needed. The formal assessment exercise is important as it is obviously better not to start a project than have to abandon it half way through.

Identifying what is needed is not always straightforward. Even if the authors are actively involved with the clinical application (and may actually use the software themselves) their approach may differ to other users and the workflow may look very different from their perspective. For example, automatic radiation dose film analysis software may speed up the process for some, but if it can't be integrated with second checks then other users may find it too difficult to use, the management may not support it or if film stops being used then the software will be a waste of time. Project Definition requires understanding of the clinical application and workflows, users, and even possible future changes. People who have "domain knowledge[iii]" are needed to help develop the user requirements. Seeking the opinions of users who will be affected by the new software can significantly reduce the risks and will help to engender a sense of "ownership" encouraging acceptance of the changes to be introduced.

A PID does not contain a full design specification – it is a high-level description of the stages required, of which detailed design is one.

A Risk Analysis should be undertaken at this stage – not of putting the software into practice (that is a later stage) but of simply undertaking the project in the first place. This requires consideration of such issues as:

- What would happen if the software was not written?
- If the software is not written, would other related projects fail?
- Is there something available commercially or in other use elsewhere that can do (most of) the job?

An initial Project Plan can then be devised (which should form part of the PID – it is often on this that the decision whether or not to proceed is made). Estimates of the actual resources are made here:

- How long (approximately), in person-days, will the project take?
- How long will it take to put the infrastructure in place?
- Are any parts of the development dependent on other tasks or resources being put in place?
- What contingencies have been made if things do not go to plan?

[ii] or PB if PRINCE 2 is being used as the controlling methodology
[iii] experts in the way things work and could work

- What documentation will be generated throughout the project, who will produce it, when will this be done, and how will it be reviewed (including QMS requirements)?
- When will the expected quality measures (e.g. code reviews) be performed and by which groups of people?
- When will the various levels of testing be performed and by whom?
- When will the system (or its constituent parts) be shown to the user?
- Which other parts of the hospital need to be involved? (MP/CE is no longer an island)

Finally, the criteria that will be used to determine the success of the project are determined and recorded in the PID, such as:

- Safety
- Availability/uptime
- Correctness
- Economy
- Optimality
- Timeliness
- Deliverability
- The expected benefits of the project (realising which may be a complete plan in itself)

Keeping It Going – Managing the Project

The PID contains an overview Project Plan (see **Error! Reference source not found.** and Figure 75 for examples), often in the form of a GANTT chart[iv]. A full plan is now required (for simple projects, the PID may have contained it). This plan outlines the way in which the project will progress, shows dependencies when multiple elements are being progressed simultaneously and gives the times at which each stage is expected to complete.

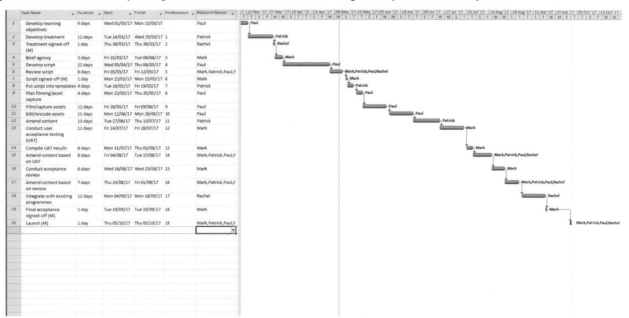

Figure 74: An Example Project Plan, from MS Project

[iv] A GANTT chart is a form of bar chart, devised by Henry Gantt in the 1910s, illustrating a project schedule. The bars describe activities: the horizontal position and length are times/durations and linkages show dependencies.

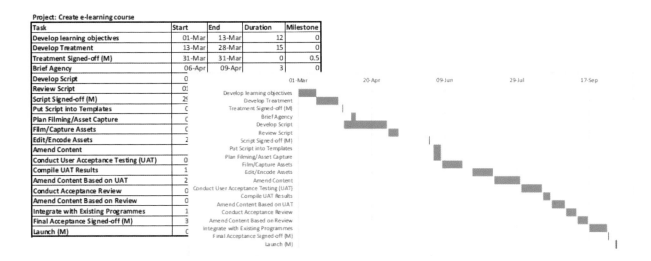

Figure 75: A Simpler GANTT Chart Created in Excel[v]

Figure 76: A GANTT Chart showing constraints

A PB consists usually of senior figures, as the PB controls the allocation of resources: it is their role to ensure the release of these, especially clinical staff time. Three major roles on the PB are therefore:

- The customer – the person who the project is for (who generally chairs the PB).
- The senior user – not necessarily someone who will use the completed project[vi], but represents staff who will and is able to control this resource (e.g. staff time for training).
- The senior technical officer – for the implementation of a commercial product, this may be someone from the supplier side. Equally it may be a shared role, if it requires technical resources from the organisation.

---

[v] : The basic instructions can be found at https:// www.ablebits.com%2Foffice-addins-blog%2F2014%2F05%2F23%2Fmake-gantt-chart-excel%2F&sa=D&sntz=1&usg=AFQjCNEOoCGcsO99Jd9DSHfCnTcDgusToQ

[vi] It is generally recognised that it is best if this person will not use the software, but is not always possible.

PRINCE 2 can seem very pedantic and focussed more on paperwork than problem solving. However, it is undoubtedly a useful tool when undertaking a complex, multi-stranded project. Simpler projects are probably better suited to a simpler method, although some elements[vii] are useful in all projects.

An often overlooked but very useful feature of project management is the sign-off. A PRINCE 2 project cannot progress from one stage to the next unless the PB completes the sign-off (agree as completed). In the TickIT[viii] methodology, the role of sign-off is given purely to the customer, who in small scale developments is the specifier, funder and end-user.

Experience shows that two of the main benefits that project management techniques can provide are:

- Sign-off: this is evidence that what has been produced is what was specified.
- The creation of a benefits expectation plan, which is vital for testing.

Stopping (the hard bit)

At the end of a project, a "lessons learned" document is produced, detailing those aspects that, with hindsight, could have been improved. This is used to inform future projects and their management.

The benefits outlined in the PID are re-examined at the end of the project to produce a Benefits Realisation Report and it is by this that the success (or otherwise) of the project is judged. If all has been successful, then the project's temporary existence is over and the software is passed into BAU for ongoing support.

Cost estimation

Whilst it is often easy to calculate the cost of delivering a project once it is scheduled (you know how many days it will take and how much those people cost, for example), that is only one part of the equation and often overlooks the true figure. A much better method is TCO, as discussed earlier (page 116).

Server- and client-side architecture

With so many methods available for delivering computerised healthcare, one major question is which one to use. Here we examine one such issue: the location of the executing software.

The term "executing software" is used in order to distinguish it from where the software actually resides and where the data resides. Indeed, it is possible to deploy systems where the data, the software and its execution are all in separate places.

The key difference is in whether the code executes on the client device or on the server. If it executes on the client, then a loss of connection is no problem, there is a lack of contention for processing power and the code can use data from the host device without it being transmitted. Additionally code may be re-used.

If the code executes on the server, then the resulting download may be smaller, confidential information residing on the server may be used and not transmitted and the server is probably a much more powerful processing device than the client. Additionally, especially for scripting, the workings of the algorithm are hidden from the end-user.

[vii] Such as benefits realisation, resource control and breaking down into stages – including the GANTT
[viii] A DTI-developed project management and certification methodology especially for software

As an example, let us consider a web page with a time and date-dependant greeting:

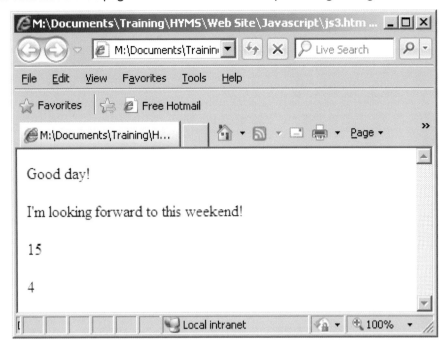

Figure 77: Web Page with a Time and Date dependant Greeting

JavaScript is client-side processing, where the web page is downloaded and the final display is generated on the client:

```
<html>
      <head>
      </head>
      <body>
            <script type="text/javascript">
                  //If the time on your browser is less than 10,
                  //you will get a "Good morning" greeting.
                  var d=new Date()
                  var time=d.getHours()

                  if (time<10)
                  {
                        document.write("<b>Good morning</b>")
                  }
                  else
                  {
                        document.write("Good day!")
                  }
                  document.write("<p>")

                  //You will receive a different greeting based
                  //on what day it is. Note that Sunday=0,
                  //Monday=1, Tuesday=2, etc.
```

```
                        theDay=d.getDay()
                        switch (theDay)
                        {
                                case 3:
                                        document.write("Woeful Wednesday")
                                        break
                                case 5:
                                        document.write("Finally Friday")
                                        break
                                case 6:
                                        document.write("Super Saturday")
                                        break
                                case 0:
                                        document.write("Sleepy Sunday")
                                        break
                                default:
                                        document.write("I'm looking forward to this weekend!")
                        }
                        document.write("</p><p>")
                        document.write(time)
                        document.write("</p><p>")
                        document.write(theDay)
                        document.write("</p>")
                </script>
        </body>
</html>
```

C++ is an example of a server-side technique, where the dynamic content is determined at the server and only the correct information for display is generated:

```cpp
time_t now=time(NULL);
struct tm *localtm=localtime(&now);
int hours=localtm->tm_hour,day=localtm->tm_wday;
cout << "<html>\n<head>\n</head>\n<body>";
if(hours<10) cout << "<b>Good morning</b>";
else cout << "Good day!";
cout << "<p>";
switch(day)
{
        case 3:
                cout << "Woeful Wednesday";
                break;
        case 5:
                cout << "Finally Friday";
                break;
        case 6:
                cout << "Super Saturday";
                break;
        case 0:
                cout << "Sleepy Sunday";
                break;
        default:
                cout << "I'm looking forward to this weekend!";
}
cout << "</p><p>" << hours << "</p><p>" << day << "</p>";
cout << "</body>\n</html>";
```

A mixture of techniques could, of course, be deployed, so that a system may take advantage of both client- and server-side processing and minimise the disadvantages. One such might be a patient monitoring system for home use: the patient's medical history is used to generate a series of criteria, without disclosing the history. These are sent to the patient's browser and the patient enters some fresh figures. These are tested using the downloaded criteria and a result given (e.g. "normal" or "contact clinic") without transmitting the actual results.

Further Reading

Clinical Engineering by Taktak, Ganney, Long & Axell: especially chapters 8-10 by Claridge, Ganney, McDonagh & Pisharody

Physics for Clinical Oncology (Radiotherapy in Practice) by Sibtain, Morgan & MacDougall: especially chapter 5 by MacDougall and Morgan.

Articles in Scope from Volume 24 onwards by Phil Cosgriff, Paul Ganney, Allan Green, Richard Trouncer and David Willis.

Project Management for Dummies

Kleinrock L, 1975-2011. Queuing Systems. Volumes 1-3. John Wiley & Sons.

Appendix 1 – List of Abbreviations

1NF – First Normal Form

2NF – Second Normal Form

3NF – Third Normal Form

ADT – Admission, Discharge and Transfer

AES – Advanced Encryption Standard

AI – Artificial Intelligence

ANSI – American National Standards Institute

ASCE – Adelard Safety Case Editor

ASCII – American Standard Code for Information Interchange

BaaS – Backup as a Service

BAU – Business As Usual

BC – Business Continuity

BNMS – British Nuclear Medicine Society

bps – bits per second

CA – Competent Authority

CAE – Claims Argument Evidence

CAPA – Corrective And Preventative Actions

CC – Change Control

CfH – Connecting for Heath

CCIO – Chief Clinical Information Officer

CDA – Clinical Document Architecture

CDEI – Centre for Data Ethics and Innovation

CDS – Clinical Decision Support

CIA – Confidentiality, Integrity and Access

CIDR – Classless Inter-Domain Routing

CIO – Clinical Information Officer

CIS – Clinical Information Systems

COTS – Commercial off-the-shelf

CPU – Central Processing Unit

CR/LF – Carriage Return/Line Feed

CSMA – Carrier Sense Multiple Access

CSV – Comma Separated Variable

CT – Computed Tomography

DaaS – Data as a Service

DCB – Data Coordination Board

DFD – Data Flow Diagram

DHCP – Dynamic Host Configuration Protocol

DICOM – Digital Imaging and Communications in Medicine

DICOM-RT – DICOM for Radiotherapy

DLL – Dynamic Link Library

DLP – Data Loss Prevention

DNS – Domain Name Service

DPA – Data Protection Act

DPO – Data Protection Officer

DPC – Data Protection Commissioner

DPIA – Data Protection Impact Assessment

DPR – Data Protection Regulator

DR – Disaster Recovery

DTI – Diffusion Tensor Imaging

EBCDIC – Extended Binary Coded Decimal Interchange Code

EDPB – European Data Protection Board

EFTA – European Free Trade Association

EHRS – Electronic Health Record System

EPR – Electronic Patient Record

EPS – Electronic Prescription Service

ER – Essential Requirement

ERD – Entity-Relation Diagram

EU – European Union

EU GDPR – The European Union General Data Protection Regulation

FD&C Act – Federal Food, Drug and Cosmetics Act

FDA – Food and Drug Administration

FDDI – Fibre Distributed Data Interface

FHIR – Fast Healthcare Interoperability Resources

FOI – Freedom of Information Act

FSN – Field Safety Notice

FTP – File Transfer Protocol

GDPR – General Data Protection Regulation

GFS – Grandfather-Father-Son

GMDD – (General) Medical Devices Directive (93/42/EEC)

GMLP – Good Machine Learning Practice

GNU – GNU Not Unix

GPO – Group Policy Object

GSN – Goal Structuring Notation

GUI – Graphical User Interface

HDF – HL7 Development Framework

HIE – Health Institution Exemption

HL7 – Health Language 7

HTTP – Hypertext Transfer Protocol

HTTPS – Hypertext Transfer Protocol Secure

HUD – Humanitarian Use Devices

IaaS – Infrastructure as a Service

ICMP – Internet Control Message Protocol

ICO – Information Commissioner's Office

IE – Information Entity

IFU – Instructions For Use

IG – Information Governance

IGSoC – Information Governance Statement of Compliance

IHMU – In House Manufacture and Use

IMAP – Internet Message Access Protocol

IMMDS – Independent Medicines and Medical Devices Safety

IOD – Information Object Definition

IP – Internet Protocol

IPEM – Institute of Physics and Engineering in Medicine

IR – Infra-Red

IRC – Internet Relay Chat

ISP – Internet Service Provider

IT – Information Technology

JAD – Joint Application Development

JDBC – Java Database Connectivity

KVP – Peak kiloVoltage

LAN – Local Area Network

LHCR – Local Health and Care Record

LPS – Left-Posterior-Superior

MAC – Media Access Control

MDDS – Medical Device Data System

MDI – Multiple Document Interface

MDIS – Medical Device Information System

MES – Medical Electrical System

MHRA – Medicines and Healthcare products Regulatory Authority

MIME - manufacture of in-house medical equipment

MLC – Multi-leaf Collimator

MPSO – Multiple Power Socket Outlet

MU – Monitor Units

NAS – Network Attached/Accessible Storage

NAT – Network Address Translation

NB – Notified Body

NDG – National Data Guardian for Health and Care

NICE – The National Institute for Health and Clinical Excellence

NNTP – Network News Transfer Protocol

NPL – National Physical Laboratory

NTP – Network Time Protocol

OAR – Organ At Risk

OBS – Output-Based Specification

OCR – Optical Character Recognition

ODBC – Open Database Connectivity

OS – Operating System

OSI – Open Systems Interconnection

OU – Organizational Unit

PaaS – Platform as a Service

PAC – Public Accounts Committee

PACS – Picture Archiving and Communications System

PAS – Patient Administration System

PAT – Portable Appliance Test

PB – Project Board

PE – Protective Earthing

PEMS – Programmable Electrical Medical System

PERT – Program Evaluation and Review Technique

PESS – Programmable Electrical Sub System

PET – Positron Emission Tomography

PGP – Pretty Good Privacy

PID – Project Initiation Document

PM – Project Management (also Project Manager)

PMA – Premarket Approval

POP – Post Office Protocol

PPM – Planned Preventative Maintenance

PPQ – Pre-Purchase Questionnaire

PRINCE – PRojects IN Controlled Environments

PSC – Patient Safety Commissioner

PT – Project Team

PTV – Planning Target Volume

QoS – Quality-of-service

QMS – Quality Management System

RAG – Red-Amber-Green

RAID – Redundant Array of Inexpensive/Independent Discs

RAM – Random Access memory

RDP – Remote Desktop Protocol

RFID – Radio Frequency Identification

RIM – Reference Information Model

RIS – Radiology Information System

ROM – Read Only Memory

RSoP – Resultant Set of Policy

SaaS – Software as a Service

SaMD – Standalone Medical Device

SA – Supervisory Authority

SAN – Storage Area Network

SCM – Software Configuration Management

SELV – Safety Extra Low Voltage

SFC – Single Fault Condition

SMTP – Simple Mail Transfer Protocol

SNMP – Simple Network Management Protocol

SONET – Synchronous Optical Network

SOUP – Software of Unknown Provenance

SQA – Software Quality Assurance

SQC – Software Quality Control

SQL – Structured Query Language

SSADM – Structured Systems Analysis And Design Method

SSH – Secure Shell

SSL – Secure Socket Layer

TCO – Total Cost of Ownership

TCP/IP – Transmission Control Protocol/Internet Protocol

TCP/UDP – Transmission Control Protocol/User Datagram Protocol

TLS – Transport Layer Security

UID – Unique Identifier

UDI-PI – Unique Device Identification-Production Identifier

UML – Universal Modelling Language

UTP – Unshielded Twisted Pair

vCPU – virtual CPU

VLAN – Virtual Local Area Network

VM – Virtual Machine

VM – Value Multiplicity

VR - Value Representation

WAN – Wide Area Network

WIMP – Windows, Icons, Mouse, Pointer – although some variants interpret "M" as "menus" and "P" as "pull-down menus"

XDS – Cross-enterprise Document Sharing

Appendix 2 – Tables and Figures

Appendix 3 – References

[1] NHS Information Governance [online]. Available: https://assets.publishing.service.gov.uk/government/uploads/system/uploads/attachment_data/file/200702/NHS_Information_Governance_Guidance_on_Legal_and_Professional_Obligations.pdf [Accessed 08/07/23]

[2] Information Commissioner's Office [online]. Available: https://ico.org.uk/for-organisations/guide-to-the-environmental-information-regulations/what-are-the-eir/ [Accessed 08/07/23]

[3] European Parliament [online]. Available: https://eur-lex.europa.eu/legal-content/EN/TXT/PDF/?uri=CELEX:32016R0679&from=EN [Accessed 08/07/23]

[4] ibid, Article 4 definition 1

[5] Information Commissioner's Office [online]. Available: https://ico.org.uk/for-organisations/guide-to-the-general-data-protection-regulation-gdpr/lawful-basis-for-processing/special-category-data/ [Accessed 08/07/23]

[6] European Parliament [online]. Available: https://eur-lex.europa.eu/legal-content/EN/TXT/PDF/?uri=CELEX:32016R0679&from=EN [Accessed 08/07/23]

[7] ibid, Article 4 definition 1

[8] Information Commissioner's Office [online]. Available: https://ico.org.uk/for-organisations/guide-to-the-general-data-protection-regulation-gdpr/what-is-personal-data/can-we-identify-an-individual-indirectly/ [Accessed 08/07/23]

[9] ibid

[10] Information Commissioner's Office [online]. Available: https://ico.org.uk/for-organisations/guide-to-the-general-data-protection-regulation-gdpr/what-is-personal-data/what-is-the-meaning-of-relates-to/ [Accessed 08/07/23]

[11] ibid

[12] European Parliament [online]. Available: https://eur-lex.europa.eu/legal-content/EN/TXT/PDF/?uri=CELEX:32016R0679&from=EN [Accessed 08/07/23]

[13] UKFast [online]. Available: https://www.ukfast.co.uk/blog/2018/07/16/gdpr-breaches-how-to-keep-them-at-bay/ [Accessed 14/08/21 – web site no longer exists]

[14] Information Commissioner's Office [online]. Available: https://ico.org.uk/for-organisations/guide-to-the-general-data-protection-regulation-gdpr/what-is-personal-data/what-is-personal-data/ [Accessed 08/07/23]

[15] ibid

[16] ibid

[17] Information Commissioner's Office [online]. Available: https://ico.org.uk/for-organisations/data-protection-reform/overview-of-the-gdpr/key-areas-to-consider/ [Accessed 08/07/23]

[18] ibid

[19] ibid

[20] Information Commissioner's Office [online]. Available: https://ico.org.uk/for-organisations/guide-to-the-general-data-protection-regulation-gdpr/what-is-personal-data/what-is-personal-data/ [Accessed 08/07/23

[21] Information Commissioner's Office [online]. Available: https://ico.org.uk/for-organisations/guide-to-the-general-data-protection-regulation-gdpr/principles/accuracy/ [Accessed 08/07/23]

[22] Kefron [online]. Available: https://www.kefron.com/blog/consent-right-forgotten-will-gdpr-affect-data-capture/ [Accessed 08/07/23]

[23] European Data Protection Board [online]. Available: https://www.europarl.europa.eu/meetdocs/2014_2019/plmrep/COMMITTEES/LIBE/DV/2019/02-25/9_EDPB_report_EN.pdf [Accessed 08/07/23]

[24] Information Commissioner's Office [online]. Available: https://ico.org.uk/for-organisations/guide-to-freedom-of-information/refusing-a-request/ exemptions [Accessed 08/07/23]

[25] Caldicott F (chair), 2013, Information: To share or not to share? The Information Governance Review [online]. Available: https://www.gov.uk/government/uploads/system/uploads/attachment_data/file/192572/2900774_InfoGovernance_accv2.pdf [Accessed 08/07/23]

[26] Information Commissioner's Office [online]. Available: https://ico.org.uk [Accessed 08/07/23]

[27] Wanley C & Cantrill K, 2013, ICT Strategy. [online]. Available: https://www.royalwolverhampton.nhs.uk/EasySiteWeb/GatewayLink.aspx?alId=11616 [Accessed 18/07/23]

[28] Snomed [online]. Available: http://www.snomed.org/ [Accessed 18/07/23]

29 *A guide to good practice for digital and data-driven health technologies*. [online]. Available: https://www.gov.uk/government/publications/code-of-conduct-for-data-driven-health-and-care-technology/initial-code-of-conduct-for-data-driven-health-and-care-technology [Accessed 18/07/23]

30 *The NHS Long Term Plan*. [online]. Available: https://www.longtermplan.nhs.uk/ [Accessed 18/07/23]

31 ibid

32 ibid

33 National Health Executive [online]. Available: https://www.nationalhealthexecutive.com/articles/department-health-social-care-publish-data-strategy-digital-transformation [Accessed 18/07/23]

34 ibid

35 19sonic92, 2010. Public domain work via Wikimedia Commons

36 ProjectManhattan, 2014. Used under creative commons license via Wikimedia Commons

37 Florian838, 2015. Used under creative commons license via Wikimedia Commons

38 Gibson Research Corporation [online]. Available: https://www.grc.com/vpn/routing.htm [Accessed 14/07/23]

39 Wikipedia [online]. Available: https://en.wikipedia.org/wiki/Port_%28computer_networking%29 [Accessed 14/07/23]

40 NHS Digital [online]. Available: https://digital.nhs.uk/data-and-information/looking-after-information/data-security-and-information-governance/nhs-and-social-care-data-off-shoring-and-the-use-of-public-cloud-services [Accessed 14/07/23]

41 NHS Digital [online]. Available: https://digital.nhs.uk/news-and-events/latest-news/two-national-nhs-services-move-to-the-cloud [Accessed 14/07/23]

42 Taktak A, Ganney PS, Long D and Axell RG, 2019, *Clinical Engineering: A Handbook for Clinical and Biomedical Engineers*, second edition. Oxford: Academic Press.

43 Kleinrock L, 1975-2011. *Queuing Systems*. Volumes 1-3. Hoboken: John Wiley & Sons.

44 Miko3k, 2007. Used under GNU license via Wikimedia Commons

45 Alexander A, 2019, Linux pipe command examples (command mashups) [online]. Available: http://alvinalexander.com/blog/post/linux-unix/linux-unix-command-mashups [Accessed 11/08/23]

46 Linus Torvalds: A Very Brief and Completely Unauthorized Biography [online]. Available: http://www.linfo.org/linus.html [Accessed 11/08/23]

47 NHSX [online] (1). Available: https://www.nhsx.nhs.uk/media/documents/NHSX_Records_Management_CoP_V7.pdf [Accessed 04/10/23]

48 NHSX [online] (2). Available: https://www.nhsx.nhs.uk/information-governance/guidance/records-management-code/ [Accessed 04/10/23]

49 Parker M, 2019, *Humble Pi: A Comedy of Maths Errors*, London: Allen Lane.

50 EdwinHelder, 2012. Used under Creative Commons License via Wikimedia Commons

51 Wikipedia [online]. Available: https://en.wikipedia.org/wiki/Session_(computer_science) [Accessed 14/07/23]

52 HL7 International [online]. Available: www.hl7.org, or www.hl7.org.uk for the UK version [Accessed 03/05/23]

53 HL7 Development Framework Project, Project Charter, HL7 2002 [online]. Available: https://www.hl7.org/documentcenter/public/wg/mnm/docs/HDF%20Project%20Charter.doc [Accessed 03/05/23]

54 Maxwell and Marciano, 2018, *What 'safety cases' mean for healthcare*, Health Service Journal [online]. Available: https://www.hsj.co.uk/topics/technology-and-innovation/what-safety-cases-mean-for-healthcare/5053463.article [Accessed 05/08/23]

55 Chambers & Associates Pty Ltd [online]. Available: http://www.chambers.com.au/glossary/hazard_log.php [Accessed 05/08/23]

56 NHS Digital, Clinical Safety documentation [online]. Available: https://digital.nhs.uk/services/clinical-safety/documentation [Accessed 05/08/23]

57 Whitbourn J, Boddy I, Simpson A, Kirby J, Farley R and Bird L, 2019, Winds of change in software regulations, Scope volume 28 issue 2

58 DICOM [online]. Available: http://www.dicomstandard.org/current/ [Accessed 03/05/23]

59 Sibtain A, Morgan A & MacDougall N, 2012, *Physics for Clinical Oncology (Radiotherapy in Practice),* Oxford: OUP

60 Law MYY, Liu B, 2009, *DICOM-RT and Its Utilization in Radiation Therapy*, RadioGraphics 29:3 [Online] Available: https://pubs.rsna.org/doi/10.1148/rg.293075172 [Accessed 03/05/23]

61 ibid

62 Systems and software engineering - Vocabulary ISO/IEC/IEEE std 24765:2010(E), 2010.

63 Sommerville I, 2007 [1982]. *Software Engineering* (8th ed.). Harlow, England: Pearson Education. p. 7. ISBN 0-321-31379-8.

64 *Software Engineering. Information Processing*. North-Holland Publishing Co. 71: 530–538. 1972.

[65] *Dictionary of Computing*, 4th Edition. Oxford: Oxford University press, p.459

[66] Knuth D, *The Art of Computer Programming: Volumes 1-4a (Box Set),* Addison Wesley

[67] British Computer Society Specialist Interest Group in Software Testing [online]. Available: http://www.testingstandards.co.uk/Component%20Testing.pdf [Accessed 11/08/23]

[68] ISO/IEC/IEEE 29119-3:2013 Software and systems engineering -- Software testing, [online] Available: https://www.iso.org/standard/56737.html [Accessed 11/08/23]

[69] Ideagen [online]. Available: https://www.ideagen.com/products/q-pulse/ [Accessed 11/08/23]

[70] PRINCE2 [online]. Available: https://www.prince2.com/ [Accessed 11/08/23]

[71] Adapted from CoFounders Lab [online]. Available: https://cofounderslab.com/discuss/is-agile-really-that-good [Accessed 11/08/23]

[72] Grady R, Caswell D, 1987, *Software Metrics: Establishing a Company-wide Program*, Hoboken: Prentice Hall. p. 159.

[73] Microsoft [online]. Available: https://msdn.microsoft.com/en-us/library/ee658094.aspx [Accessed 15/08/23]

[74] TickIT [online]. Available: http://www.tickitplus.org/ [Accessed 15/08/23]

[75] Codd EF, 1970, *A Relational Model of Data for Large Shared Data Banks*, Association for Computing Machinery (ACM,) Vol. 13, No. 6, June 1970, pp 377-387

[76] *Dictionary of Computing*, 1996, Fourth Edition. Oxford: Oxford University Press.

[77] Wellkang Tech Consulting [online]. Available: http://www.ce-marking.org/Guidelines-for-Classification-of-Medical-Devices.html [Accessed 15/08/23]

[78] Official Journal of the European Union L117 Volume 60, 5 May 2017 [online]. Available: http://eur-lex.europa.eu/legal-content/EN/TXT/?uri=OJ:L:2017:117:TOC [Accessed 15/08/23]

[79] Loh E and Boumans R, 2017, *Understanding Europe's New Medical Devices Regulation*, Emergo [online]. Available: https://www.emergogroup.com/resources/articles/whitepaper-understanding-europes-medical-devices-regulation [Accessed 15/08/23]

[80] Official Journal of the European Union L117 Volume 60, 5 May 2017 [online]. Available: http://eur-lex.europa.eu/legal-content/EN/TXT/?uri=OJ:L:2017:117:TOC [Accessed 15/08/23]

[81] ibid

[82] ibid

[83] ibid

[84] Loh E and Boumans R, 2017, *Understanding Europe's New Medical Devices Regulation*, Emergo [online]. Available: https://www.emergogroup.com/resources/articles/whitepaper-understanding-europes-medical-devices-regulation [Accessed 15/08/23]

[85] ibid

[86] ibid

[87] MEDICAL DEVICES: *Guidance document – Qualification and Classification of stand alone software (MEDDEV 2.1/6),* European Commission [online].Available: http://www.meddev.info/_documents/2_1_6_ol_en.pdf [Accessed 15/08/23]

[88] MHRA [online]. Available: https://www.gov.uk/guidance/medical-devices-conformity-assessment-and-the-ukca-mark [Accessed 15/08/23]

[89] *The Medical Devices (Amendment etc.) (EU Exit) Regulations 2020*, UK Government [online]. Available: https://www.legislation.gov.uk/ukdsi/2020/9780348213805/memorandum/contents [Accessed 15/08/23]

[90] *Businesses given more time to apply new product safety marking*, UK Government [online]. Available: https://www.gov.uk/government/news/businesses-given-more-time-to-apply-new-product-safety-marking [Accessed 15/08/23]

[91] Stewart H, 2023, *The Brexit 'red tape' illusion has been exposed by the Tories' CE mark climbdown*, The Guardian, 1/8/23.

[92] NHSX [online], 2023, The NHS AI Lab. Available: https://www.nhsx.nhs.uk/ai-lab/ [Accessed 15/08/23]

[93] Medicines and Healthcare products Regulatory Agency [online], 2023, Good Machine Learning Practice for Medical Device Development: Guiding Principles. Available: https://www.gov.uk/government/publications/good-machine-learning-practice-for-medical-device-development-guiding-principles/good-machine-learning-practice-for-medical-device-development-guiding-principles [Accessed 15/08/23]

[94] FDA [online]. Available: https://www.fda.gov/about-fda/what-we-do [Accessed 15/08/23]

[95] FDA [online]. Available: https://www.fda.gov/medical-devices/general-hospital-devices-and-supplies/medical-device-data-systems [Accessed 15/08/23]

[96] FDA [online]. Available: https://www.fda.gov/MedicalDevices/ProductsandMedicalProcedures/DeviceApprovalsandClearances/ [Accessed 15/08/23]

[97] MHRA [online]. Available: https://www.gov.uk/government/organisations/medicines-and-healthcare-products-regulatory-agency/about [Accessed 15/08/23]

[98] MHRA [online]. Available: https://www.gov.uk/government/organisations/medicines-and-healthcare-products-regulatory-agency [Accessed 15/08/23]

[99] Gartner [online]. Available: http://www.gartner.com/it-glossary/total-cost-of-ownership-tco/ [Accessed 04/08/23]

[100] Carr A S, Smeltzer L R, 1997, *An empirically based operational definition of strategic purchasing,* European Journal of Purchasing and Supply Management 3 (4), 199–207.

[101] Lysons K and Farrington B, 2016, *Procurement and Supply Chain Management*, London: Pearson Education

[102] RadekK, 2007, used under Creative Commons Attribution-Share Alike 3.0 Unported license via Wikimedia Commons

[103] Wikipedia [online]. Available: https://en.wikipedia.org/wiki/Cloud_computing [Accessed 25/08/23]

[104] von Neumann, J, 1949, *Theory and organization of complicated automata,* In Burks AW (Ed. and completed), 1966, *Theory of self-reproducing automata.* Urbana: University of Illinois Press.

[105] Rivest R, Shamir A, Adleman L, 1978, *A Method for Obtaining Digital Signatures and Public-Key Cryptosystems,* Communications of the ACM. 21 (2): 120–126. doi:10.1145/359340.359342.

[106] Clay Mathematics Institute, The RSA algorithm [online]. Available: http://www.claymath.org/posters/primes/rsa.php [Accessed 07/06/12 – link now broken, even on their website!]

[107] Stanford University [online]. Available: https://cs.stanford.edu/people/eroberts/courses/soco/projects/2004-05/cryptography/pgp.html [Accessed 01/07/23]

[108] Kishore A, 2015, What is a Checksum and How to Calculate a Checksum [online]. Available: https://www.online-tech-tips.com/cool-websites/what-is-checksum/ [Accessed 01/07/23]

[109] Parker M, 2015, *Things to Make and Do in the Fourth Dimension*, London: Penguin, p.346.

[110] National Health Executive, 2018, *NHS cyber-attack fears return as all tested trusts fail assessments* [online]. Available: http://www.nationalhealthexecutive.com/Health-Care-News/nhs-cyber-attack-fears-return-as-all-tested-trusts-fail-assessments [Accessed 25/08/23]

[111] Cburnett, 2006. Used under GNU license via Wikimedia Commons

[112] IEC Standard 82304 [online]. Available: https://www.iso.org/standard/59543.html [Accessed 04/10/23]

[113] IEC 60601-1:2006+A12:2014

Printed in Great Britain
by Amazon

32359980R00094